FAMILY LENTEN HANDBOOK
CHANGE MY HEART

PAULIST PRESS
New York, N.Y./Ramsey, N.J.

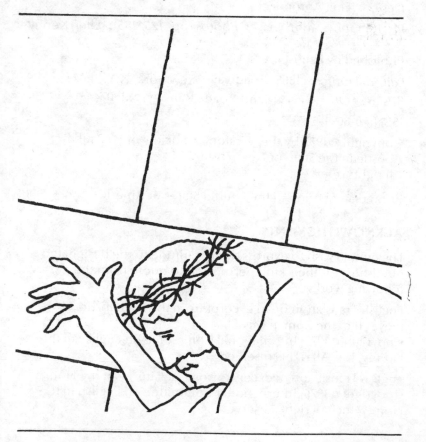

The *Family Lenten Handbook*
is a component of
CHANGE MY HEART, A Parish Lenten Program

General Editor:
Jean Marie Hiesberger
with Bernadette Kenny, R.S.H.M. and Robert Heyer

Editorial Assistant: Gerald Twomey, C.S.P.

Design: Emil Antonucci

Photography: John Glaser *Photos (pp. 125, 135):* Ellen Kenny

Published by Paulist Press

Editorial Office: 1865 Broadway New York, N.Y. 10023

Business Office: 545 Island Road Ramsey, N.J. 07446

ISBN: 0-8091-9173-3

ACKNOWLEDGMENTS

The editors wish to express their gratitude to the designated
publishers for their kind permission to quote from the
following works:

English Translation of an excerpt from the Eucharistic
Prayer II of the Roman Missal.
Copyright ©1973, International Committee on English in the
Liturgy, Inc. All rights reserved.

English Translation of excerpts from the Liturgy of the Hours.
Copyright © 1975, International Committee on English in the
Liturgy, Inc. All rights reserved.

CONTENTS

THE WAY OF THE CROSS FOR FAMILIES
Sr. Mary Hopkins, O.P.

INTRODUCTION

Lent is a time of renewal and repentance for injustice or sin; it is a time of being born again. During Lent we are invited to take a look at our lives, to weigh our relationship with Christ our friend, and Savior, with our families, friends and all humankind. The whole process of renewal and repentance, rebirth requires a willingness to die to self in order that we may rise new and changed persons. For each one of us, our dyings and risings come in our everyday lives, with those people who share our lives. Often that death to self comes through a giving to others, giving of our time, our lives and our feelings. In and through prayer we share most deeply our relationship with God and with one another.

By reflecting together on the meaning of the passion of Jesus in their own lives, families will be strengthened and renewed. "The Way of the Cross for Families" is a basis for such reflection.

Lent is a time for journeying. The Way of the Cross symbolizes life's journeys. The journey is a long process. Families should decide at the beginning of Lent how they will reflect on this journey. They may decide to reflect on one station of the cross each evening during Passion week and Holy week or they may decide to reflect on two each week of Lent beginning with Ash Wednesday. Whatever decision is made, it is important that sufficient time be given to the prayer so that each member of the family may enter into the journey.

Plan For Family Prayer

a. Reading

This is a brief account of a particular station. Family members may take turns reading it. Whoever reads it should have prepared beforehand and read it slowly and carefully.

b. Reflection and Discussion

Pause for a moment of silent prayer and reflection on the reading. Each member of the family is then invited to share what the reading meant to him/her. The points for "reflection" are offered as a discussion guide.

c. Create a Station

As a family, create the stations you are reflecting on. This may be done in a variety of ways. Some suggestions are: 1) Cut out magazine pictures and paste them on cardboard to show one way in which people today might experience this station. 2) On sheets of paper draw the station. 3) On sheets of paper draw ways that we experience this station today. 4) Make a list of ways that this station happens today. 5) Using clay make a symbol of this station. A different way of creating the station may be used each time. Just be sure to have the necessary materials ready so that the creation of the station is part of the prayer service and not an interruption.

d. Prayer Shared Together

Your prayer may be silent or voiced. Each person in the family has the opportunity to say what he/she feels, in his/her own words to Jesus who is there present in the midst of the family gathered in His name in prayer.

e. Resolution

End each prayer experience by a resolution to do something as a family. The resolution should be both practical and possible of attainment; e.g. this week we will try to be conscious of people who feel down. We will try to encourage them. While making the resolution, you may wish to light a candle and hold hands around the table. The resolution may be written right in this book after each station. In this way, you will have a family record of how your family brought life out of the dyings of every day.

f. Concluding Prayer

This prayer read by a member of the family may conclude the family prayer service. Families may wish to substitute a song in place of the concluding prayer or family members could take turns being responsible for writing their own concluding prayers.

THE FIRST STATION: JESUS IS CONDEMNED TO DEATH

a. Reading

Pilate called together the chief priests, the ruling class, and the people and spoke to them saying: "You have accused this man Jesus of subverting the people. Having examined him in your presence I can find no charge against him arising from your charges. Therefore I intend to release him once I have taught him a lesson." But the crowd cried out, "Away with this man; release Barabbas!" Barabbas was in prison for causing an uprising in the city, and for murder. Pilate again spoke to the crowd as he wanted Jesus to be the one released. "What wrongdoing is this man guilty of? I cannot find anything about him that calls for the death penalty." But they demanded with loud cries, "Crucify him, crucify him!" Pilate then ordered what the crowd demanded be done. He released Barabbas, the one they asked for, who had been thrown in prison for insurrection and murder and Jesus he had scourged and handed him over to be crucified. (Luke 22:13-25)

b. Reflection

How very much alone you must have felt, Jesus, when the

crowd laughed and shouted at you.

How do we sometimes treat others as the crowd treated you?

How can we become more loving and accepting of one another?

c. Create a Station
Show how this station is experienced today.

d. Shared Prayer
Express your prayer to the Lord who is present among you.

e. Resolution
_____

_____

f. Concluding Prayer
Lord Jesus, as we walk with you on the Way of the Cross, help us to see you in each of our brothers and sisters. Teach us to love and accept one another. Help us not to condemn others by what we say or do. Listen to our prayer and come to our help, Lord.

THE SECOND STATION: JESUS ACCEPTS THE CROSS

a. Reading
The soldiers stripped Jesus of his clothes and dressed him in a scarlet military cloak. They weaved a crown out of thorns, put it on Jesus' head, and stuck a reed in his hand. Then they laughed at him, saluting him with, "All hail, King of the Jews!" and pretending to pay him homage. They also spat at him and taking hold of the reed, struck him with it. Finally, they stripped Jesus of the cloak, dressed him in his own clothes and led him away carrying the cross. (Mark 15:16-21)

b. Reflection

Jesus carried the heaviest of all crosses. Most of our crosses are nothing more than small trials.

Do we accept our crosses or make them heavier by complaining about them?

How can we help others to accept their crosses?

c. Create a Station

Show how this station is experienced today.

d. Shared Prayer

Express your prayer to the Lord who is present among you.

e. Resolution

_____

_____

f. Concluding Prayer

Jesus, help us to follow you by carrying our cross daily, especially during this time of Lent. Give us courage to accept whatever suffering is ours and to see it as a means of growing closer to you. We believe that you are our resurrection and our life. Give us your Spirit as the source of our life and help us to work for what is pleasing to you.

THE THIRD STATION: JESUS FALLS THE FIRST TIME

a. Reading

The scourging and crowning with thorns were very painful and made Jesus extremely weak. Carrying the cross to Calvary caused even greater pain and weakness. Jesus took each painful step out of love for us, pain and weakness which eventually caused him to fall under the weight of the cross.

b. **Reflection**
Jesus was willing to suffer for us, even to the point of falling under the weight of a cross.

Are we willing to suffer with and bear the weight of our crosses?

How can we help others, especially those in our family when they fall?

c. **Create a Station**
Show how this station is experienced today.

d. **Shared Prayer**
Express your prayer to the Lord who is present among you.

e. **Resolution**

_____

_____

f. **Concluding Prayer**
Help us, Jesus, to be aware of and sensitive to others who carry heavy crosses. Deepen within each of us a love that reaches out to help others when they fall. We too at times stumble under the burden of our own personal crosses. Stay close to us, Jesus. We cannot go on without you. Thank you for your love, for the example that you are.

THE FOURTH STATION: JESUS MEETS HIS AFFLICTED MOTHER

a. **Reading**
The words of Simon to Mary of long ago, "This child is destined to be the downfall and the rise of many in Israel, a sign that will be opposed and you yourself shall be pierced with a sword, so that the thoughts of many hearts may be

laid bare," are now brought to fulfillment. What great sorrow filled Mary's heart and how it must have hurt her to witness such injustice toward her son. Once again Mary is called in faith to accept this time of trial as part of God's plan for her.

b. Reflection
How can we be open and ready to accept the will of God in our lives each day?

c. Create a Station
Show how this station is experienced today.

d. Shared Prayer
Express your prayer to the Lord who is present among you.

e. Resolution

_____

_____

f. Concluding Prayer
Lord Jesus, the great "Yes" of both you and your Mother Mary carried you throughout the whole of your lives right to this moment. Grant that we might take our example from your "Yes" to life. Make us holy. Holy Mary, Mother of God, pray for us sinners, that we may believe and follow in the path of you and your son.

THE FIFTH STATION: SIMON HELPS JESUS CARRY THE CROSS

a. Reading
A man named Simon of Cyrene was coming in from the fields and met Jesus carrying the heavy cross. The weight of the cross had weakened Jesus so that the guards feared Jesus would not make it to the place of crucifixion, so they forced Simon to help Jesus carry the cross. A crossbeam was

put on Simon's shoulder for him to carry along behind Jesus.

b. Reflection
Simon helped Jesus in his time of need.

Do we willingly reach out to help those in need or do we ignore them as though they were not present to us?

Is there someone in need of our help right now and what can we do to help that person?

c. Create a Station
Show how this station is experienced today.

d. Shared Prayer
Express your prayer to the Lord who is present among you.

e. Resolution

_____

_____

f. Concluding Prayer
Lord Jesus, deepen our faith so that we may see you in others and come to your aid. Help us to be holy people of God by doing good for those in need. Teach us to pray in time of trouble and need, for you always answer us. We praise and thank you for saving us and calling us to be your holy people.

THE SIXTH STATION: VERONICA WIPES THE FACE OF JESUS

a. Reading
As Jesus walked to Golgotha, the place of crucifixion, He met many among whom He had preached and taught about His Father. Some of these people cared deeply about Jesus

and were filled with great sorrow to see Him suffering so. One woman, Veronica, realizing the pain that Jesus was in, stepped out from the crowd and gently wiped the face of Jesus. How grateful Jesus was for what might seem to be a very small act but at the same time was a most courageous act and more importantly, an act of great love.

b. Reflection

Veronica didn't think of herself and what others might think of her but was sensitive to the suffering Jesus.

Have we lessened or added to the sufferings of others this day?

Are we grateful to others especially members of our family when they reach out to help us or do we treat them with indifference?

How can we be a source of comfort and support to one another in our family?

c. Create a Station

Show how this station is experienced today.

d. Shared Prayer

Express your prayer to the Lord who is present among you.

e. Resolution

_____

_____

f. Concluding Prayer

Lord, teach us to be sensitive to the needs of others and to believe that you are present in the simple things as well as in the great works of the universe. Give us an openness to others that shows itself in acts of courage and love. Because we share the love and strength of the other members of our family, may our love for one another support us in trying times, Lord.

THE SEVENTH STATION: JESUS FALLS THE SECOND TIME

a. Reading
The cross weighed heavily upon Jesus and at times caused Him to fall to the ground. Each time He fell the soldiers forced the cross upon Him again. Out of love for us, He rose to His feet and went on.

b. Reflection
To some the fall of Jesus was considered failure but Jesus was strong in time of failure and did not become easily discouraged.

What is our response to our own failures and the failures of others?

How can we be more like Jesus in responding to failures?

c. Create a Station
Show how this station is experienced today.

d. Shared Prayer
Express your prayer to the Lord who is present among you.

e. Resolution

_____

_____

f. Concluding Prayer
Lord Jesus, we pray for your strength to meet failure and to not become easily discouraged by it. Help us too, to support others with love and understanding in their failures. Continue to guide and direct us during this Lenten Season

and if we have failed to keep some of our Lenten promises help us to remember, Lord, that it is never too late to begin again. Thank you for the great love that you have for each of us, Jesus.

THE EIGHTH STATION: JESUS SPEAKS TO THE WOMEN OF JERUSALEM

a. Reading
Many people followed Jesus as He walked the road to Calvary. Among the crowd of people were some women who were weeping because Jesus was in such pain and being treated so unjustly. Jesus looked kindly upon them and said: "Women of Jerusalem! Do not cry for me but rather for yourselves and for your children." Great as Jesus' personal pain was, He was attentive to those around him.

b. Reflection
Even in His own agony, the suffering of others touched Jesus.

Did we today ignore the sufferings of others so we would not have to become involved?

Did we refuse to listen and respond to someone around us suffering?

Is there someone who is poor to whom we can respond in a concrete manner?

c. Create a Station
Show how this station is experienced today.

d. Shared Prayer
Express your prayer to the Lord who is present among you.

e. Resolution

_____

_____

f. Concluding Prayer
Lord Jesus, grant that your example and our own suffering may teach us to respond to the sufferings of others in a loving and helping manner. Help us to see suffering when out of convenience we would rather ignore it and to listen to those who need our help. Give us your Spirit to strengthen, guide and direct us in all we do.

THE NINTH STATION: JESUS FALLS THE THIRD TIME

a. Reading
Having suffered other falls, it became increasingly difficult for Jesus to rise up and stand and continue walking. Once again however, Jesus stood and continued on the way of the cross suffering unjust pain and insults.

b. Reflection
How very great Jesus' love for us is. Does His suffering mean anything to us personally or is it just a fact of history?

Are we prepared to suffer for the good of others?

What does the example of Jesus say to us?

c. Create a Station
Show how this station is experienced today.

d. Shared Prayer
Express your prayer to the Lord who is present among you.

e. Resolution

_____

_____

f. Concluding Prayer
Jesus, after each fall you struggled to your feet and continued to walk the way of the cross even though this brought increased pain. Thank you for loving us. Teach us to follow your example by continuing on when life seems difficult. Let us never forget that no fall is too great if we once again turn to you and find courage and strength. You are the Son of God, our Savior. We believe in you.

THE TENTH STATION: JESUS IS STRIPPED OF HIS GARMENTS

a. Reading
When Jesus arrived at Golgotha, the place of crucifixion, the few possessions He had by way of clothing were taken from Him. Later the soldiers took Jesus' clothes and divided them into four parts, one part for each soldier. The robe that Jesus wore was made from one piece of woven cloth and the soldiers didn't wish to tear it so they threw dice to see who would get it.

b. Reflection
The soldiers attempted to take from Jesus all that He had but they could not take His love. When our thoughts and ideas are rejected do we respond in love?

Are we willing to be separated from personal possessions in order to help those less fortunate?

c. Create a Station
Show how this station is experienced today.

d. Shared Prayer
Express your prayer to the Lord who is present among you.

e. Resolution

_____

_____

f. Concluding Prayer
Thank you, Jesus, for your constant love even in the face of rejection and physical pain. Help us never to lose our love for others even though the personal cost may at times seem great. Instill within us your peace to help us through difficult times. Give us eyes to see and compassion for your poor. Guide us in a loving response to them, Lord. Thank you for being our Savior and calling us to be holy.

THE ELEVENTH STATION: JESUS IS NAILED TO THE CROSS

a. Reading
When they arrived at the place of crucifixion Jesus was nailed to the cross. An inscription proclaiming His offense read, "The King of the Jews"; this was placed over His head. People who passed by insulted and laughed at Jesus saying such things as, "Save yourself by coming down from the cross." The chief priests and scribes also joined in and taunted Him: "He saved others but He cannot save Himself! Let the Messiah, King of Israel come down from the cross now, so we can see and believe in Him." This led Jesus to pray, "Father, forgive them; they do not know what they are doing."

b. Reflection
In our family we at times have need to forgive one another.

We need to take an example from Jesus who in His final agony prayed for forgiveness for those who persecuted Him.

Let us at this time offer one another some sign of peace and forgiveness.

c. Create a Station
Show how this station is experienced today.

d. Shared Prayer
Express your prayer to the Lord who is present among you.

e. Resolution
_____

_____

f. Concluding Prayer
Jesus, strengthen us to share in your suffering by our obedience to God's will. Help us to be a forgiving people and to rejoice when you forgive any of your sons and daughters. Free us from the slavery of sin during this time of Lent and let us always be true to you. We praise you and give you glory.

THE TWELFTH STATION: JESUS DIES ON THE CROSS

a. Reading
From noon onward, there was darkness over the whole land that lasted until midafternoon. Toward midafternoon Jesus cried out in a loud voice, "Eli, Eli, lama sabachthani?" which means, "My God, my God, why have you forsaken me?" Some of the bystanders remarked, "Listen! He is calling on Elijah!" Then one of them ran off and got a sponge. He soaked it in cheap wine and sticking it on a reed, tried to make Jesus drink. Others said, "Leave Him alone. Let's see whether Elijah comes to take Him down." Then Jesus

cried out in a loud voice, "Father, into your hands I commend my spirit," and breathed His last. A soldier, upon seeing the manner of Jesus' death, gave glory to God by saying, "Surely this was the Son of God!" (Mark 15:33-39)

b. Reflection
Spend some quiet time reflecting upon the death of Jesus. Consider the price He was willing to pay for truth and for His great love for each of us.

c. Create a Station
Show how this station is experienced today.

d. Shared Prayer
Express your prayer to the Lord who is present among you.

e. Resolution

_____

_____

f. Concluding Prayer
Lord Jesus, through your sufferings and death you have taken away our sins, healed our offenses and touched us with your deep and everlasting love. With you, we now entrust our lives into the hands of our Father, praying that we might always remain in His care. All glory be to you, the Father and Holy Spirit, Amen.

THE THIRTEENTH STATION: JESUS IS TAKEN DOWN FROM THE CROSS

a. Reading
As evening drew near, Joseph from Arimathea, one of Jesus' disciples and one who looked forward to the reign of God, went to Pilate to request the body of Jesus. Pilate was surprised to learn that Jesus had already died so he called one

of the soldiers to inquire as to whether or not Jesus had died. Upon learning that Jesus was dead, Pilate gave Joseph permission to remove Jesus' body from the cross. He took it down and following Jewish burial custom wrapped it in fine linen with perfumed oils. (John 18:38-40)

b. Reflection
In spite of many doubts Joseph of Arimathea had no doubt about the eventual reign of God. Jesus was now dead, but Joseph continued to show love for the One he followed.

How do we meet the demands of love especially in time of doubt?

Do we remember that love is kind, patient, neither jealous nor self-seeking?

Does our love lead us to do what we know is right?

c. Create a Station
Show how this station is experienced today.

d. Shared Prayer
Express your prayer to the Lord who is present among you.

e. Resolution

_____

_____

f. Concluding Prayer
Lord Jesus, we believe that you are God's own Son and that you suffered and died for us in order to save us. Open our ears and hearts to your word especially in time of doubt so that we may always remain true to you in love.

THE FOURTEENTH STATION: JESUS IS LAID IN THE TOMB

a. **Reading**
   Near the place where Jesus had been crucified was a garden in which there was a new tomb carved out of the rock. Joseph of Arimathea took Jesus' body which he had wrapped in fine linen and buried it there. Then he rolled a huge stone in front of the tomb and went away; some women who had followed him remained there for a time before going home to observe the sabbath as a day of rest. (John 18:41:42)

b. **Reflection**
   In the spirit of the day, reflect quietly on Jesus' passion, death and promise of resurrection. The sufferings and death are only part of our reflection. On the third day, God our Father raised the lifeless body of Jesus to new life.

   He now lives forever to lead us to the Father. How well do we follow?

c. **Create a Station**
   Show how this station is experienced today.

d. **Shared Prayer**
   Express your prayer to the Lord who is present among you.

e. **Resolution**
   _____

   _____

f. **Concluding Prayer**
   God our Father, today is a day of waiting. We know that Jesus has risen from the dead. We rejoice in that fact. Oftentimes though we are called to wait not knowing what is going to happen, just as Jesus' friends did not know. At times we even feel alone and frightened. Help us always to

keep before our eyes the gift of Jesus your Son and the presence of your Spirit. Grant that our love for one another may support us in difficult times.

Give the stations of the cross that the family has made a prominent place in your home and on Easter Sunday incorporate the account of the Resurrection which should include a reading of the account from Scripture, a reflection upon it and spontaneous family prayer.

THE STATIONS OF THE CROSS

Jim Janda, S.J.

INTRODUCTION

Love, love, love, and remember that you were loved even before you were created. For God who sees himself, passionately loves the beauty of his creation, and he created it because his love is boundless, to give it eternal life and allow it to enjoy the indescribable blessedness which he himself possesses. (Catherine of Siena)

It is hoped that this little series of meditations on the Stations of the Cross bring all a feeling of God's great love.

I would suggest that parents and children gather for one Station an evening. The opening prayer and meditation could be recited antiphonally. The entire family is invited to share in the suggested dialogue, and close with a prayer of their choosing.

Most important is the dialogue where we may hear Christ speaking to us through the other—each must listen to the suffering Christ speaking through the other.

PRAYER

Father,
>   you created all things good,
>   you created nothing hating it,
>   you created all things out of love.

So great was your love for us that
>   even though you foresaw all of our mistakes,
>   even though you foresaw all of our failures,
you said, Let it be.

So great is your love for us that
>   you will not notice our mistakes,
>   you will not notice our failures,
but only our goodness—you keep giving life.

And because we cannot believe your love,
>   you sent us your Son,
and because we cannot believe your love,
>   you send us your Spirit
to remind us of your tender loving kindness.

Teach us to spend our lives
>   as Christ did—healing and forgiving,
help us to pull out the weeds in our hearts
>   which choke out his words of life,
teach us to be grateful for the gift of life
>   in ourselves and others,
>   in all that you have made.

Father,
>   you created all things good,
>   you created nothing hating it,
>   you created all things out of love.

JESUS IS CONDEMNED TO DEATH

The earth is God's garden
    and like the flowers and trees,
we are meant to grow, bloom,
    and die in his love.

Each of us is like a seed
    we bear God's secret,
what each of us is meant to be.

We find this out by praying
    as Jesus did.
He prayed in the desert
    and often
he went off alone to pray.

. . . when you pray, go to your private room and, when you
have shut your door, pray to your Father who is in that secret
place, and your Father who sees all that is done in secret will
reward you. (*Matthew 6, 5-6*)

That is what Jesus said,
that is how we find out
what the Father wants
each of us to be.

Jesus was condemned to death
    for being what he was meant to be:
Others could not accept this,
    others could not believe this.

We condemn ourselves to death
    when we cannot accept ourselves

as we are—for what we are.

Jesus tells us,

I am happy
  with you,
as you are,
  for what you are.

My suffering and
death
prove this.

Love yourself
  as I love you,
and remember
  if you do,
my Father and I
  and the Holy Spirit
will make our home
  in you.

Dialogue:
What do I hate about myself?
Do I realize God loves me as I am?

Each person could tell one thing
they like about each member of
the family.

JESUS ACCEPTS HIS CROSS

From that time Jesus began to make it clear to his disciples that
he was destined to go to Jerusalem and suffer grievously at the

hands of the elders and chief priests and scribes, to be put to death and to be raised up on the third day. Then, taking him aside, Peter started to argue with him. "Heaven preserve you, Lord," he said; "this must not happen to you." But he turned and said to Peter, "Get behind me, Satan! you are an obstacle in my path, because the way you think is not God's way but man's." *(Matthew 16, 21-23)*

Jesus knew that he would have to suffer and die.

Each of us as friends of Jesus must suffer and die a little, sometimes each day.

Jesus asks us,

Can you believe
that I show my love
for you
both in good times
and in hard times?

Can you believe
that I am just
as close to you
in suffering
as when all things
are going well?

The Father knows
what is best for you.

He provides for
the sparrow and
field lily.

He will strengthen
you
as he strengthened
me.

Dialogue:
What is something you have suffered?
How have you come closer to Jesus
through the suffering?

JESUS FALLS THE FIRST TIME

A chestnut that you can hold
        in the palm of your hand
will grow so tall and so wide
        you will not be able
to put your arms around it
        or touch the top of it.

But that will take many years
        and the growing tree
will have to see many springs,
        summers, falls, and winters
before it can become what it
        was meant to be—
that secret, hidden in its seed.

We can learn faith
and patience
from the chestnut tree.

At this time the disciples came to Jesus and said, "Who is the
greatest in the kingdom of heaven?" So he called a little child

to him and set the child in front of them. Then he said, "I tell you solemnly, unless you change and become like little children you will never enter the kingdom of heaven. And so, the one who makes himself as little as this little child is the greatest in the kingdom of heaven." *(Matthew 18, 1-4)*

A child cannot survive alone,
a child has a lot to learn.
Christ in this story is telling us,
you cannot survive alone,
you have a lot to learn.

Part of learning is making mistakes,
part of learning is failing,
part of learning is getting discouraged.

If we try to follow Christ
    we will fail,
if we try to follow Christ
    we will make mistakes.

He understands this.
    If we fall, he will help us.
Jesus tells us,

My children,

*I know you have
made mistakes.*

Look,

*I have fallen
under my cross.*

I want to carry it,
but it is too heavy
and I am so weak,
but I will try.

I know you have
heavy things to
carry too.

Let me help you.

Dialogue:
What are some heavy burdens
that make us fall?

What mistakes discourage us?

JESUS MEETS HIS MOTHER

Now the hour has come
for the Son of Man to be glorified.
I tell you, most solemnly,
unless a wheat grain falls on the ground and dies,
it remains only a single grain;
but if it dies,
it yields a rich harvest.
Anyone who loves his life loses it;
anyone who hates his life in this world
will keep it for the eternal life. (*John 12, 23-25*)

If we see a beautiful flower,
        we want to pick it.
If we meet a good person,
        we want to be with him.

If we are having a party,
     we take snapshots of the family
     and friends to make it last
     forever
It is hard to let go.

That is part of what it means
     to be human—
not wanting to let go.

That is what it means
     to die—
to let go.

Every time we let go
     of someone or some thing,
we die a little,
     that is part of our cross,
     that is part of being human.

But empty hands can be filled.
     The Father will never
cease to bless us with
     friends and good things—
but only if we let go.

Mary's child was a gift,
     she did not keep him,
     she gave him to us,
     she "let go."

Mary tells us,

My child was a gift

of love.
He was not given to me
   to keep.
I have given him
   to you
so you might understand
   the Father's
love.

Because I let him
   die for you,
he could rise for you
   and give you
new life.

Dialogue:
What are some ways we die a little
each day?

What was some "new life" you found
after "letting go"?

SIMON HELPS JESUS CARRY HIS CROSS

Squirrels store and provide
      for themselves.
You can watch them burying nuts,
      and in fall
carrying fresh leaves
      in their mouths up the tree
and into their hole.

But the sparrows—

they are creatures of trust.
They don't know when
    someone will throw them
a crumb—yet people do—
    and the sparrows survive.

Look at the birds in the sky. They do not sow or reap or gather
into barns; yet your heavenly Father feeds them. Are you not
worth much more than they are? Can any of you, for all his
worrying, add one single cubit to his span of life? . . . So do
not worry about tomorrow: tomorrow will take care of itself.
Each day has enough trouble of its own. (*Matthew 6, 26, 27, 33, 34*)

Simon helps Jesus carry his cross.
Jesus turns to us and says,

Look,
    my cross is too heavy,
    I cannot carry it
    any farther,
but
    in my weakness
    my Father
    sends me Simon.

Just as my Father
    helped me,
he will help you.

He will send
    friends and
    strangers
to help you.

Dialogue:
Can you remember any friends
or strangers who helped you?

On the street, at work, at
school?

How did it make you feel?

VERONICA WIPES THE FACE OF JESUS~

A legend tells that while Christ was carrying his cross, a woman
named Veronica, moved to pity, wiped the sweat from his face
with a towel. As a reward for her kindness, Christ caused his
face to be imprinted on the towel.

If anyone gives so much as a cup of cold water to one of these
little ones because he is a disciple, then I tell you solemnly, he
will most certainly not lose his reward. (*Matthew 10, 42*)

The Gospels show us time and time again
that little things matter.

Mother Teresa of Calcutta once said that
at Mass, Christ is hidden in the bread,
but at work he is hidden in the neighbor.

Christ wishes us peace, happiness, joy,
not confusion, bitterness, and anxiety.
Whenever we are thoughtful of another,
even in the smallest way, we are carrying
on his work and wishes.

Dialogue:
What are some little things

others have done to us which
have made us happy and brought
us joy?

What have I done to bring joy to
someone else?

JESUS FALLS AGAIN

Your salvation lay in tranquility,
your strength in complete trust.
(*Isaiah 30, 15*)

Does a woman forget her baby
        at the breast,
or fail to cherish the son
        of her womb?
Yet even if these forget
I will never forget you.
(*Isaiah 49, 15*)

Lord, my heart will live for you,
my spirit will live for you alone.

You will cure me and give me life,
my suffering will turn to health.

It is you who have kept my soul
from the pit of nothingness.

You have thrust all my sins
behind your back.
(*Isaiah 38, 16-17*)

If a seed is planted,
if it is watered,
if it is warmed by the sun,
    it will grow and bloom,
    it will become
    what it was meant to be.

If stones are piled on the seed,
    it may sprout, but it will die.

Like the seed
    we will become our secret
    if we are loved,
but if we are burdened with
    the stones of guilt, worry, and fear,
we cannot grow
    or become Christ to others.

Jesus fell under the weight of his cross.
We may fall under the weight of guilt,
        fear, and worry.

Jesus knew we would be burdened
        with many things
that is why he said,

Come to me, all you who labor and are overburdened, and I
will give you rest. Shoulder my yoke and learn from me, for I
am gentle and humble in heart, and you will find rest for your
souls. Yes, my yoke is easy and my burden light. *(Matthew 11,
28-30)*

Christ has forgiven us,
we must forgive ourselves.

Dialogue:
What are some of our burdens?

Why are we afraid to share them
with one another or ask for help?

JESUS MEETS THE WOMEN

It is told that Jesus comforted the women of Jerusalem who
wept when they saw him. Jesus who often quoted the
prophets, may have recalled the words of Yahweh to Isaiah,
"Comfort my people, comfort them."

It is such a little thing
　　　to ask someone how they are doing,
　　　or how their day went, or to listen
　　　to their problems.
Such a little thing,
　　　always possible, always close at hand,
　　　but so difficult at times to do.

Teresa of Avila reminds us of the
　　　importance of doing the possible,
　　　common, everyday things when
　　　she says,

I told you elsewhere that the devil sometimes puts ambitious
desires into our hearts, so that, instead of setting our hand to
the work which lies nearest to us, and thus serving Our Lord in
ways within our power, we may rest content with having
desired the impossible. Apart from praying for people, by
which you can do a great deal for them, do not try to help
everybody, but limit yourselves to your own companions . . .
(Peers, E. Allison, (ed.). *The Complete Works of Saint Teresa of
Jesus*, Vol. II, Page 349. New York: Sheed and Ward, 1944.)

Dialogue:
How can we imitate Christ and
Isaiah in comforting people?

How would you like to be comforted?

JESUS FALLS THE THIRD TIME

If we say we have no sin in us,
we are deceiving ourselves
and refusing to admit the truth;
but if we acknowledge our sins,
then God who is faithful and just
will forgive our sins and purify us
from everything that is wrong.
To say that we have never sinned
is to call God a liar
and to show that his word is not in us.
(*1 John 2, 8-10*)

Peter denied Jesus three times,
but later became his true friend
and died for him.

We are all sinners,
but we are forgiven.
Can we believe this?

Jesus fallen under
the weight of his cross
looks up to us and says,

I am doing this
for you

because I love you.

*Why can't you
believe me?*

*I know you have sinned.
Come back to me.*

*Remember, before you
were born
I saw all the good
you would do
and
I saw all the evil
you would do,*

*but I loved you
so much
I gave you life.*

*Please don't get
discouraged,
come back to me
with all your heart.*

Dialogue:
A family forgiveness service.

Each could think of the ways
in which they hurt the other
members, and ask forgiveness.

JESUS IS STRIPPED OF HIS CLOTHES

The stripping of Jesus was a public humiliation.
   He bore it, he had known sadness before.

The Pharisees constantly tried to
   trick Jesus with questions.
      He could have let distrust
      grow in his heart—he did not.

The lepers whom he had cured
   did not return to thank him.
His disciples often advocated
   hatred and violence
   in spite of his teaching;
      yet he would not let
      depression grow in his heart.

The thought of his suffering and death
   terrified him,
      but he cried out to the Father;
      he would weed out the despair
      he felt in his heart.

To be human means
   to find distrust, depression, despair
   in our heart—but to weed it out,
for the Father did not put it there.

Saint Ignatius tells us that the devil
   wishes us distrust, doubt, confusion
   and despair,
But Christ wishes us joy, peace, patience
   in suffering.

Dialogue:
What are those weeds in our hearts
that would choke out God's joy and
peace in us?

Who are the people in our lives
that cause us sadness?

Can we forgive them?

JESUS IS NAILED TO THE CROSS

Pity, compassion, gentleness,
    marked Christ's life.

He prayed to the Father—
    and listened to the Spirit
    speaking in his heart.

He spent his life,

    building up, not tearing down
    loving, not hating

    bringing peace, not confusion
    forgiving, not holding grudges

    speaking kindly, not spitefully
    healing, not harming

    seeking truth, not the lie
    bringing life, not death.

Jesus was condemned to death

for being what he was meant to be;
others could not accept this,
    others could not believe this.

Saint Paul who died for Christ
    has these encouraging words for us
    who try to live as Christ lived,

Do not let your love be a pretense, but sincerely prefer good
to evil. Love each other as much as brothers should, and have a
profound respect for each other. Work for the Lord with
untiring effort and with great earnestness of spirit. If you have
hope, this will make you cheerful. Do not give up if trials
come; and keep on praying. If any of the saints are in need you
must share with them; and you should make hospitality your
special care. (*Romans 12, 9-13*)

Dialogue:
Whom have I caused to suffer?
Whom have I nailed to a cross
by my hatred?

JESUS DIES

Take this, all of you, and drink from it:
this is the cup of my blood,
the blood of the new and everlasting covenant.
It will be shed for you and for all men
so that sins may be forgiven.
Do this in memory of me.
(*From Eucharist Prayer 2* Copyright © 1973, International
Committee on English in the Liturgy, Inc. All rights reserved.)

Our worst enemies are loved by God,
those who have hurt us are loved by God,
the entire act of creation was and is
a movement of love, he created nothing
hating it.

Can we believe this and forgive as
Christ did?

John of Cronstadt suggests a Christ
attitude toward the sinner,

Every person that does any evil . . .
is sufficiently punished by the evil
he has committed . . . but chiefly by
the fact that he withdraws himself from
God: it would therefore be insane and
most inhuman to nourish anger against
such a man; it would be the same as
to drown a sinking man, or push into
the fire a person who is already being
devoured by the flame. To such a man,
as to one in danger of perishing, we
must show double love, and pray
fervently to God for him; not judging
him, not rejoicing at his misfortune.
(Fedotov, E. P., ed. *A Treasury of Russian Spirituality.* New
York: Sheed & Ward, 1948. Page 402)

Jesus says,

You must
*   forgive others*
as I have
*   forgiven you.*

I know this
   will be difficult,
but remember,

Ask
   and you shall receive,
seek
   and you shall find,
knock,
   and the door shall
   be opened to you.

Dialogue:
Whom do I find difficult to forgive?
How can I begin to forgive them?

JESUS IS TAKEN DOWN FROM THE CROSS

Jesus moved out toward others
   with love and respect
   wanting to lighten others' burdens.

The Pharisees moved out toward others
   with hate and violence
   placing crushing burdens on others.

Judas moved into himself
   with hatred and violence
   destroying himself—a gift
   from the hand of the Father.

Each of us moves in all three
   of these ways—
and Jesus knew we would.

He hoped, however, that we would
   try more and more to live as he did—
moving out toward others with love and respect,
   wanting to lighten their burden.

He knew we would fail,
   but he could accept this.

He hoped we would not
   abandon him because of personal failure
but that we would keep trying
   and praying for help
for he knew the power to perform
   our task in life would be given.

We are only the earthenware jars that hold this treasure, to make it clear that such an overwhelming power comes from God and not from us. We are in difficulties on all sides, but never cornered; we see no answer to our problems, but never despair; we have been persecuted, but never deserted; knocked down, but never killed; always, wherever we may be, we carry with us in our body the death of Jesus, so that the life of Jesus, too, may always be seen in our body.

Dialogue:
Try to think of one person who
has many burdens.

What can you do to lighten one
of them?

JESUS IS BURIED

Discouragement,
failure,

hating ourselves,

these can bury
us and keep us
from following
Christ.

Christ will never
    abandon us,
Christ will never
    throw us away,
Christ does not
    want death,
but life, full and
    abundant.

The white blood cells in the blood stream have the task of
locating, isolating, and engulfing things harmful to the life of
the human body. They destroy invading bacteria or neutralize
the poisons.

We too must isolate, locate, and destroy those poisons in
ourselves which would be harmful to the human community.

And this task
    is a labor of love;
love for the family,
    love for the community,
love for Christ.

It is the only worthwhile
    occupation—
it must be felt in
    the marrow,
it is the reason for

Christ's life and death,
it is the cause of creation.

Love is always patient and kind; it is never jealous; love is
never boastful or conceited; it is never rude or selfish; it does
not take offense, and is not resentful. Love takes no pleasure in
other people's sins but delights in the truth; it is always ready
to excuse, to trust, to hope, and to endure whatever comes.
(1 Corinthians 13, 4-8)

Dialogue:
What are some of our failures?
What makes us discouraged?

CHRIST RISES

The shell
　of the seed
protects new
　life until
　it is ready
　to root and
　stretch out
　its arms
to its Maker.

The cocoon
　which binds
　and hides
is only meant
　to house
　new life
till it is
ready to fly.

Who could see
   the blue
   green and
   gold of the
peacock's tail
   if he did
   not break
out of the egg?

We may find ourselves
   enclosed in
      worry and fear
      hatred and despair
      bitterness and
      discouragement
but these things
   are meant to be
      grown out of.

For a new life in Christ
   to rise with him
      and become
      what the Father
      is calling
      each one to be
in the Spirit
in community.

OUR FATHER

   (always child)
Lord of the Dance
      child of games

I have heard your

laughter
running to hide

and am not afraid

in cocoons
caterpillars dream
the unbelievable

Let us listen to Christ
according to John.

My little children,

Do not let your hearts be troubled.
Trust in God still, and trust in me.

whoever believes in me
will perform the same works as I do myself,
he will perform even greater works

If you ask for anything in my name,
I will do it.

. . . the Holy Spirit,
whom the Father will send in my name,
will teach you everything
and remind you of all I have said to you.

Do not let your hearts be troubled or afraid.

Make your home in me, as I make mine in you.

If you remain in me
and my words remain in you,

you may ask what you will
and you shall get it.

You did not choose me,
no, I chose you;

The father will give you
anything you ask him in my name.

In the world you will have trouble,
but be brave:
I have conquered the world.
(*John: 14:1, 12, 14, 26, 27; 15:4, 7, 16; 16:33*)

Dialogue:
What are some things each of us
would like to grow out of?

How can we support and help
one another in this?

CONCLUSION

Christ has something
    very special in mind
    for each of us.
The secret was hidden
    in our seed,
as we grow
    we come to know this.

Christ wishes us
    new life—

"I have come to make
    all things new,"
he said.

If we can keep
    trying to live
in his love,
    he will surprise
us in many ways.

And when he calls us
    from this earth,
the first thing we
    will want to tell him,
face to face, will be,
    not, "I'm sorry,"
    but, "Thank you, Lord,
    for everything!"

EVENING PRAYER FOR LENT

Rev. William Bauman

**An Evening Prayer Service
for use in early Lent**

Leader: God, come to my assistance.
All: Lord, make haste to help me.
Leader: Glory to the Father, and to the Son, and to the Holy
     Spirit:
All: as it was in the beginning, is now, and will be for ever.
     Amen.
All: Man cannot live on bread alone but by every
     word that comes from the mouth of God.

Magnificat:

Leader: My soul proclaims the greatness of the Lord,
     my spirit rejoices in God my Savior
     for he has looked with favor on his lowly servant.
All: From this day all generations will call me blessed:
     the Almighty has done great things for me,
     and holy is his Name.
Leader: He has mercy on those who fear him
     in every generation.
All: He has shown the strength of his arm,
     he has scattered the proud in their conceit.
Leader: He has cast down the mighty from their thrones,
     and has lifted up the lowly.
All: He has filled the hungry with good things,
     and the rich he has sent away empty.
Leader: He has come to the help of his servant Israel
     for he has remembered his promise of mercy,
     the promise he made to our fathers,
     to Abraham and his children for ever.

All: Glory to the Father, and to the Son, and to the Holy Spirit:
as it was in the beginning, is now, and will be for ever.
Amen.

All: Man cannot live on bread alone but by every
word that comes from the mouth of God.

Leader: Let us give glory to Christ the Lord, who became our
teacher and example and our brother. Let us pray to
him saying:
Lord Jesus, you became like us in all things but sin;
teach us how to share with others their joy and sorrow,

All: that our love may grow deeper every day.

Leader: Help us to feed you in feeding the hungry,

All: and to give you drink in giving drink to the thirsty.

Leader: You raised Lazarus from the sleep of death,

All: grant that those who have died the death of sin may
rise again through faith and repentance.

Leader: Inspire many to follow you with greater zeal and
perfection,

All: through the example of the Blessed Virgin Mary and the
saints.

Leader: Let the dead rise in your glory,

All: to enjoy your love for ever.

All: Our Father . . .

Leader: Lord our God,
you formed man from the clay of the earth
and breathed into him the spirit of life,
but he turned from your face and sinned.
In this time of repentance
we call out for your mercy.
Bring us back to you
and to the life your Son won for us
by his death on the cross,
for he lives and reigns for ever and ever.

All: Amen.

Leader: May the Lord bless us,
　　　protect us from all evil
　　　and bring us to everlasting life.
All: Amen.

A Celebration of Evening Prayer
for the First Sunday of Lent
or some evening in early Lent

Leader: God, come to my assistance.
All: Lord, make haste to help me.
Leader: Glory to the Father, and to the Son, and to the Holy
　　　Spirit:
All: as it was in the beginning, is now, and will be for ever,
　　　Amen.

Song

Psalmist: Lord God, we ask you to receive us
All:　and be pleased with the sacrifice we offer
　　　you this day with humble and contrite hearts.
Ps: I have called to you, Lord; hasten to help me!
　　　Hear my voice when I cry to you.
　　　Let my prayer arise before you like incense,
　　　the raising of my hands like an evening oblation.
All: Set, O Lord, a guard over my mouth;
　　　keep watch at the door of my lips!
　　　Do not turn my heart to things that are wrong,
　　　to evil deeds with men who are sinners.
Ps: Never allow me to share in the feasting.
　　　If a good man strikes or reproves me it is kindness;
　　　but let the oil of the wicked not anoint my head.
　　　Let my prayer be ever against their malice.
All: Their princes were thrown down by the side of the
　　　rock;
　　　then they understood that my words were kind.

As a millstone is shattered to pieces on the ground,
    so their bones were strewn at the mouth of the grave.
Ps: To you, Lord God, my eyes are turned:
    in you I take refuge; spare my soul!
    From the trap they have laid for me keep me safe:
    keep me from the snares of those who do evil.
All: Glory to the Father, and to the Son, and to the
    Holy Spirit:
    as it was in the beginning, is now, and will be for
    ever. Amen.
All: Lord, God, we ask you to receive us
    and be pleased with the sacrifice we offer you this day
    with humble and contrite hearts.
Leader: Lord, from the rising of the sun to its setting your
    name is worthy of all praise. Let our prayer come like
    incense before you. May the lifting up of our hands be as
    an evening sacrifice acceptable to you, Lord our God.
Ps: Christ died for all sins,
    the innocent for the guilty to bring us back to God.
All: In the body he was put to death, but in the spirit he was
    raised to life.
Ps: Though he was in the form of God,
All: Jesus did not deem equality with God something to be
    grasped at.
Ps: Rather, he emptied himself
All: and took the form of a slave, being born in the likeness of
    men.
Ps: He was known to be of human estate,
All: and it was thus that he humbled himself,
    obediently accepting even death,
    death on a cross!
Ps: Because of this, God highly exalted him
All: and bestowed on him the name above every other name.
Ps: So that at Jesus' name every knee must bend
All: in the heavens, on the earth, and under the earth,

and every tongue proclaim to the glory of God the Father:
JESUS CHRIST IS LORD!

Ps: Christ died for our sins,
the innocent for the guilty to bring us back to God.

All: In the body he was put to death, but in the spirit he was
raised to life.

Leader: Listen to us, O Lord, and have mercy, for we have
sinned against you.

All: Listen to us, O Lord, and have mercy, for we have sinned
against you.

Leader: Christ Jesus, hear our humble petitions,

All: For we have sinned against you.

Leader: Glory to the Father, and to the Son, and to the Holy
Spirit.

All: Listen to us, O Lord, and have mercy, for we have sinned
against you.

Song

All: Our Father . . .

Leader: The Lord be with you.

All: And also with you.

Leader: May Almighty God bless you,
the Father, and the Son, and the Holy Spirit.

All: Amen.

Leader: Go in peace.

All: Thanks be to God.

Evening Prayer for Use in Late Lent

Leader: God, come to my assistance.

All: Lord, make haste to help me.

Leader: Glory to the Father, and to the Son, and to the Holy
Spirit:

All: as it was in the beginning, is now, and will be for ever.
Amen.

All: I will thank the Lord with all my heart
　　　in the meeting of the just and their assembly.
　　　Great are the works of the Lord
　　　to be pondered by all who love them.
　　　Majestic and glorious his work,
　　　his justice stands firm for ever.
　　　He makes us remember his wonders.
　　　The Lord is compassion and love.
　　　He gives food to those who fear him;
　　　keeps his covenant ever in mind.
　　　He has shown his might to his people
　　　by giving them the lands of the nations.
　　　His works are justice and truth:
　　　his precepts are all of them sure,
　　　standing firm for ever and ever:
　　　they are made in uprightness and truth.
　　　He has sent deliverance to his people
　　　and established his covenant for ever.
　　　Holy his name, to be feared.
　　　To fear the Lord is the first stage of wisdom;
　　　all who do so prove themselves wise.
　　　His praise shall last for ever!

Leader: Merciful and gentle Lord, you are the crowning glory
　　　of all the saints. Give us, your children, the gift of
　　　obedience which is the beginning of wisdom, so that we
　　　may do what you command and be filled with your mercy.

Leader: Let us stand and together praise God in the Magnificat
　　　(see services for early Lent for spoken and sung versions).

Ant. When I am lifted up from the earth,
　　　I will draw all people to myself.

Leader: All praise to God the Father who brought his chosen
　　　people to rebirth from imperishable seed through his
　　　eternal Word. Let us ask him as his children:
　　　God of mercy, hear the prayers we offer for all your
　　　people.

All: May they hunger for your word more than for bodily
　　food.
Leader: Give us a sincere and active love for our own nation
　　and for all mankind,
All: may we work always to build a world of peace and
　　goodness.
Leader: Look with love on all to be reborn in baptism,
All: that they may be living stones in your temple of the Spirit.
Leader: You moved Nineveh to repentance by the preaching
　　of Jonah,
All: in your mercy touch the hearts of sinners by the preaching
　　of your word.
Leader: May the dying go in hope to meet Christ their judge,
All: may they rejoice for ever in the vision of your glory.
All: Our Father . . .
Leader: Father,
　　help us to be like Christ your Son,
　　who lived the world and died for our salvation.
　　Inspire us by his love,
　　guide us by his example,
　　who lives and reigns with you and the Holy Spirit,
　　one God, for ever and ever.
All: Amen.
Leader: May the Lord bless us,
　　protect us from all evil
　　and bring us to everlasting life.
All: Amen.

Evening Prayer for Use in Late Lent

Song
Leader: Happy the man who shows mercy for the Lord's sake;
　　(Psalm 112)

All: he will stand firm forever.

Leader: Happy the man who fears the Lord,
who takes delight in all his commands.
His sons will be powerful on earth;
the children of the upright are blessed.

All: Riches and wealth are in his house;
his justice stands firm for ever.
He is light in the darkness for the upright:
he is generous, merciful and just.

Leader: The good man takes pity and lends,
he conducts his affairs with honor.
The just man will never waver:
he will be remembered for ever.

All: He has no fear of evil news;
with a firm heart he trusts in the Lord.
With a steadfast heart he will not fear;
he will see the downfall of his foes.

Leader: Open-handed, he gives to the poor;
his justice stands firm for ever.
His head will be raised in glory.

All: The wicked man sees and is angry,
grinds his teeth and fades away;
the desire of the wicked leads to doom.

Leader: Glory to the Father, and to the Son, and to the
Holy Spirit:

All: as it was in the beginning, is now, and will be forever.
Amen.

Leader: Happy the man who shows mercy for the Lord's sake;

All: He will stand firm forever.

Leader: Lord God, you are the eternal light which illumines
the hearts of good people. Help us to love you, to rejoice
in your glory, and so to live in this world as to avoid
harsh judgment in the next. May we come to see the light
of your countenance.

Song

Leader: We worship you, O Christ, and we praise you.

All: We worship you, O Christ, and we praise you.

Leader: Because by your cross you have redeemed the world.

All: We praise you.

Leader: Glory to the Father, and to the Son, and to the Holy Spirit.

All: We worship you, O Christ, and we praise you.

Leader: Before his passion, Christ looked out over Jerusalem and wept for it, because it had not recognized the hour of God's visitation. With sorrow for our sins, let us adore him and say: You longed to gather to yourself the people of Jersualem, as the hen gathers her young,

All: Teach all peoples to recognize the hour of your visitation.

Leader: Do not forsake those who have forsaken you.

All: Turn our hearts to you, and we will return to you, Our God.

Leader: Through your passion you gave grace to the world,

All: Help us to live always by your Spirit, given to us in baptism.

Leader: By your passion, help us to deny ourselves.

All: And so prepare to celebrate your resurrection.

Leader: You reign in the glory of the Father.

All: Remember those who have died today.

All: Our Father . . .

Leader: Almighty, ever-living God,
you have given the human race Jesus Christ our Savior
as a model of humility.
He fulfilled your will
by becoming man and giving his life on the cross.
Help us to bear witness to you
by following this example of suffering
and make us worthy to share in his resurrection.

Leader: May the Lord bless us,

protect us from all evil
and bring us to everlasting life.
All: Amen.

ALL THE WAY TO EASTER

A Journey of Forty Days
Mary Louise Tietjen

Some wandered in desert wastes
   finding no way to a city to dwell in;
hungry and thirsty,
   their soul fainted within them.
Then they cried to the Lord in their trouble,
   and he delivered them from their distress;
he led them by a straight way,
   till they reached a city to dwell in.
(Psalm 107)

Lent is our "straight way," and it leads not to a city but to a person, the person of the Risen Lord. His gift is more than a Promised Land. It is the great promise that all ages have yearned to hear: You too shall rise with me.

So let us set out. . . .

The Lent of former years was preceded by Shrovetide, a three-day period set apart for confession—(to be shriven was to be freed from sin). Thus the great penitential season that followed was actually a living out of the prescribed sacramental penance. (It was Shrove Tuesday before it was Mardi Gras!) Does it not seem logical to begin, rather than conclude, our Lent with the Sacrament of Reconciliation?

● Daily bread for this journey? The Eucharist, if at all possible. No other Lenten "sacrifice" approaches this.

● Speaking of daily bread, we could say grace before and after each meal we share, not just a Sunday dinner or holiday feast, but the everyday meal which is the high point of each day. This provides a "graceful" beginning and ending.

● To give up something, to abstain from something edible, is a most practical—and difficult—penance. It is humbling, it is amazing to find how hard it is to refrain from an item of "mere food." We do indeed realize it is Lent when we omit butter or desserts or cigarettes, or morning coffee, or the cream and sugar in it.

● And then there is my friend who fasted for forty days from both coffee and the morning newspaper.

● Here is a penance that might not be a penance at all to half the population, but in a night-owl family it would be a great sacrifice: lights out at least half an hour earlier than usual each Lenten evening. (See how much nicer you are to each other the next day, even if you missed the TV special.)

● You know that neighbor on the block whom no one likes? Find a way to be friendly. (OK. No one said this was going to be easy.)

● To emphasize the journey aspect of Lent, have your household pilgrims find pictures of great highways, little paths, footprints in sand, winding roads, etc. Mount these on construction paper for home display.

● Have you ever wanted to begin a steady regime of scripture-reading? Now is the acceptable time. Even better: read with two or three friends during each week of Lent.

● Next door is a teen-age girl who makes it a Lenten practice to choose and read new bedtime stories to a much younger sister. Do yourself a favor and rediscover the children's room of any public library.

● Small children in the family will wish that Lent would never end if an older child or adult plays checkers with them or teaches them a simple card game on Friday nights.

• Early spring is the traditional make-new, clean-up time in almost every home. Such a renewal is very becoming to Lent. Let each person be responsible for putting fresh paper in dresser drawers, cleaning his or her own closet, dusting the door top, scrubbing the window sill—all the extra cleaning projects of the season.

Older members can sort their outgrown clothes to be passed on to others. In one large household, it is the rule: nothing new for Easter until all the old have been tried on, decided upon, straightened up.

After such a wardrobe overhaul, why not a family (or neighborhood) mending night, refurbishing the give-aways with proper buttons and snaps, repairing torn seams and drooping hems? Make an event of this ending with doughnuts and milk. Let older members show younger ones the special tacking stitch that makes for invisible hems. And younger ones can demonstrate to an older generation an imaginative embroidered blue-jeans patch.

In the "good old days," one member of such a group always read while the others sewed. Here's a challenge: could you come up with a reading that would amuse and interest (say, for twenty minutes) your group of needle-workers? Might not be so difficult as reaching family agreement on the evening's TV channel.

• Once when my children were small, the father in this family had to be away for two months. It was lonely, but lightened unexpectedly when a good friend called to say, "I'm going to come over and mend with you every Tuesday night." She did and it was great and I got to the bottom of the bag for the first time in a year. Come to think of it, that was during Lent. Somehow, I hoped I wasn't her "penance"!

• To consider: other religions of the world have their fasts, their seasonal times of penance. For Moslems, many of them desert nomads, there is the month-long Ramadan, with each day's complete fast broken only at sundown (and then one feasts!). The prophet's last message to his people was:

Remember that faith is in the heart. He who keeps the fasts, but does not abandon lying and slandering, God does not care about his leaving off eating and drinking!

● The Jews also annually recall their exodus from slavery, their Shrovetide (and subsequent long journey)—in the festival of Passover. This is the great redeeming act through which the Lord delivered Israel from bondage and established his people, foreshadowing the greater Passover from death to life eternal.

An exodus is a going-out, a leave-taking of the habitual, the familiar. Let families at this time talk about an exodus they experienced, what it was such as a move to a new home. Let children recall what it was like going away to camp for the first time. Let us remember grandparents and great-grandparents who made their passage across the ocean to the New World. They looked forward with great expectations; yet, it was such a wrench, such a departure from everything known and dear to them.

Find a map of the Exodus route (many Bibles carry a map section)—traditionally through the Sinai Desert, extremely arid, with few oases, but many steep bare red granite peaks. Let a young geographer make a large simplified graph for the family bulletin board. On another map, let him or her trace, with a broad felt marker, the route by which your family came to its own "Land of Milk and Honey."

● Something to talk about: Easter has many loving names: The Sunday of Joy, High Sunday, the First of Days, the Feast of Feasts. But in every language—except English and German!—Easter in fact is known as Passover (Pasque—Pasen—Paskha—Päske—Pascua, etc.). Ask older family members or friends to tell of their paschal customs in other times, perhaps in other lands.

● For forty years, the Israelites lived in tents, as wanderers, learning to become the Lord's people. If you are a camping family, plan a weekend under canvas for a memorable Lenten experience. Watch the stars together, the same stars that patterned the skies above the Covenant People.

● There are many fine books that tell the Exodus story for young persons. One with excellent illustration and interesting historical notes is *The Long Journey* by Lichtveld and Bouhuys, New York: Paulist/Newman Press, 1969.

● Lent is indeed a time to learn. And it was *the* learning time for earlier catechumens, their period of immediate preparation for Baptism. Their initiation is one of the great Lenten themes.

● Reactivate in your home a small holy water font. Why do we have a font at the entrance to the church, at the doorway of a room? Its primary reason for being is as a reminder of our Baptismal day—and the water passage that marked our entrance to the Church.

● If you have any "white garments of Baptism" in the family, show them again during Lent. Have a family guessing game: how many other "sign garments" can you count?

Formerly the white garment of the newly baptized was worn throughout Easter Week. But everyone in the community also wore something new to rejoice with the newcomers, and in memory of one's own white-garment time. Let us wear—with this awareness—our new Easter clothes.

Does your parish prepare "white garments" for its new members? Perhaps this Lent might be the time to pioneer such an endearing and meaningful program. Be sure that the garment is accompanied by an explanation of its significance—printed or typed attractively.

● Ask that the names of these new members be published as a welcome in the parish bulletin.

● A plant, foliage or blooming, is a just-right Easter gift. It says something about the green and radiant land that waits for us after the desert journey. It speaks of the Lord who came back to us in a garden, who died that he might lead his people into another Eden.

● Is there a green thumb among you? I have a friend who annually roots many, many little African violets (under fluorescent light on the ping-pong table in her basement) as Easter gifts for her many, many friends.

● If the youngsters in the family want to make their own Easter greetings, give them old seed catalogues with their glorious flower pictures. Cut out and mount in little folders—with a message. (Remember to size the folder to fit a standard envelope.)

● Passion Sunday/Palm Sunday brings us within sight of journey's end. We carry our palm leaves home and place them in a tall narrow vase in a stairway window—they are symbols for all the descents and ascents of this week.

● Pilgrims to the Holy Land in other days were known as "palmers": they often wore a palm leaf as a sign of the completed journey. We modern palmers see our Palm Sunday sign as a promise, the promised happy ending of our lifelong pilgrimage.

"The just man shall flourish like the palm tree."

Lord, you are our Living Water. Only near you can we flourish and grow.

● Easter is a movable feast; it follows a lunar, not a solar calendar. It is celebrated on the first Sunday following the first full moon after the vernal equinox (March 21). So on a clear night during Holy Week, assemble outside to view the full moon that set the date for this year's Easter!

● This is a week during which it is good to speak of death with our families, of how there are appointed times for all things. Let us examine our own faith in the Resurrection; let us re-think our own feelings and reactions to death in the light of the great promise.

● To consider: People throughout the ages have longed for the certainty of life after death—and the survival of personal identity. The ancient Egyptians had no doubts concerning the after-life. Carefully they prepared the body in yard upon yard of linen windings; with much ritual they laid it in the tomb. But a great banquet awaited the returning mourners, and they cel-ebrated! The departed was on his way to a happy life that would never end—and so he was toasted in fine wine, songs were sung in his praise, and all spoke his name with joy. In a certain way, such a funeral seems more Christian than ours.

● There is a sign that through the centuries has been one of mystery, of new life, of spring itself (emerging from the closed bud, the closed shell, the closed tomb)—a sign of resurrection dear to the Chinese, the Persian, the Greek, the Jew. What is it? The Easter egg!

Do you know there is a special blessing for Easter eggs?

"We beseech thee, O Lord, to bestow thy blessing upon these eggs, to make them a wholesome food for thy peo-ple, who gratefully partake of them in honor of the resur-rection of Our Lord Jesus Christ."

Eggs were once a highly acceptable Easter gift because the Lenten fast of early days prohibited eggs as well as meat, milk, butter, and cheese. But during our current Lent, with eggs allowed and plentiful, why cannot the Julia Childs among us have a cooking class for our beginners? Let them learn how to make

egg salad
deviled eggs
poached eggs
and baked-custard-with-a-sprinkle-of-nutmeg.

● And there is symbolism to be enjoyed in a home-baked loaf for Holy Thursday.

● Dyeing Easter eggs is fun for all ages. Make a celebration of this; try to find a time when various ages can be present. Older family members will remember tricks and designs for Easter eggs that will delight the younger. Others should gather a few Christian symbols to adorn very special eggs.

To be ready, let the homemaker prepare the white boiled eggs *early* in Holy Week. If you have been "making Easter" for a family for many years, the following lore is in your bones. But if you're new at it, perhaps you'll be glad for the following hints:

a) buy medium or small white eggs—the more to dye, the merrier.

b) start room-temperature eggs in cool water. No refrigerated eggs in hot water if you want any uncracked eggs left to color.

c) use a large glass or enamel pan (an old dish pan is great). Lower eggs in with a slotted spoon. A dish towel on the botton helps to

d) bring the water slowly to a boil, then simmer till hard-boiled. How long? At least twenty minutes *after* the water boils, and even then, test one egg before removing all.

e) rinse cooked eggs in cold water—to keep the yolk from darkening and to provide a smooth clean surface.

f) refrigerate till party time.

● And so at last it is our Rainbow Day, the Day of ancient promise, like the rainbow day that spoke to Noah. All colors are gathered in white and all colors are Easter colors.

● Let a large white candle burn in your home at Eastertide, just as the Easter candle lights the sanctuary. Place a ring of fresh greens at the base of the Christ Candle.

And for the day after? For Easter Monday? This was once the

time appointed for the parish boundary walk, to mark off ancient limits and boundary lines. This was once the day all townspeople walked out together to admire the spring. And in many parts of the world, it is still the traditional day to visit grandparents.

And this is the day for a picnic! (Remember the deviled eggs . . .)

The Lord of all things lives anew
And all his works are living too!
Alleluia! Alleluia!

("The World Itself" by John M. Neale 1818-66)
The Book of Holidays, N.Y., Thomas Y. Crowell, 1958,
by J. Walker McSpadden, page 62.

PREPARING A HOME MASS
Bernadette Kenny, R.S.H.M.

Traditionally Lent is a time set aside for renewal and reform. We seek to change ourselves and to deepen the meaning and purpose of our lives. As Christians we know that we cannot do this by ourselves or in isolation from one another. We are called to faith, in the context of a community. This community is called to be a community of believers. Just as each one of us needs renewal and changes so too does the entire community.

As a community we need to deepen and renew our relationship to the Lord and to one another. One of the best ways of doing this is through the community's central action of worship—the mass. The celebration of the Lord's supper both presupposes a community and helps to build a community. It also helps to renew a community.

It is not the mere fact of going to mass which renews the community. The idea reduces the mass to a magic formula. It is rather the rich experience of a community at worship which is renewing. One way of helping people to have this rich experience is by providing the opportunity for a home mass. Mass in the home offers a more intimate setting for the community's prayer. Fewer people in a smaller place helps us to realize that we are indeed a community of people who believe that Jesus is Lord and that when we celebrate this supper in memory of him he is present in our midst. Having a home mass also makes more evident to us the link between our everyday lives and our faith.

Good liturgy, a good community experience, whether it be at home or in the church requires planning. For some of us liturgy planning is a relatively new experience. This is no reason to panic or to think we are not capable of having a mass in our homes. We have all had some experience of planning a celebration or a party or a meal for company. Thinking about the process we go through in planning a celebration gives us a clue to planning a home mass.

When we plan a party we ask ourselves questions like: What are we celebrating? What do we do which demonstrates the event that we are celebrating? With whom do we wish to celebrate this event? What atmosphere do we wish to have dominate this celebration? What will contribute to this atmosphere? These same questions will help us plan a home mass.

WHAT ARE WE CELEBRATING?

In the Eucharistic liturgy we are celebrating something which is a great value to us—our faith. We are celebrating our belief that we are called to share in the life of the Lord.

Faith has many dimensions. It is a gift from God. It is a gift which grows as we grow. It is expressed in action. It is a loving relationship with the Lord. It involves dying and rising with the

Lord not just as a thing of the past but in our everyday lives. These are just a few of the dimensions of our faith.

Because our faith is so rich, we need to choose one aspect of it for our celebration. Just as a family would have difficulty celebrating a wedding, a baptism, a homecoming and a funeral all at one time, we would have difficulty trying to celebrate all the aspects of the great mystery of our redemption at once. The liturgical year takes a whole year to celebrate the many aspects of this mystery and then we do this continually throughout our lives.

So we need to choose an aspect of faith or a theme for our celebration. There are several ways of going about this. If we know most of the people who will be coming to the mass, we can pick a theme which will be meaningful to them. We can pick a theme that the parish has been concentrating on during this Lenten season or if we are going to use the readings from the mass of the day, we can use the theme of these readings as our mass theme. In this case we need to pray over the readings and to discern the theme.

HOW DO WE DEMONSTRATE THE THEME?

It is hard to imagine a birthday party without a cake and candles. We don't just say "Happy Birthday," we do something which shows that we are grateful for the person we are celebrating. So too with our faith. We don't just say over and over again we believe. We need to ritualize our belief—to demonstrate our faith in a prayerful manner.

The Liturgy of the Word is a particulary appropriate place to ritualize or demonstrate the theme of our celebration. Once readings are chosen, we need to ask ourselves: How can we best communicate the theme of these readings? In order to communicate with the people of his own day, Jesus spoke their language, used images that were familiar to them. In order to hear God's word in our time, we need to hear it in our language. It is not enough to say our language is English or French or Spanish. Our language is a visual one. In a sense we hear not only with our ears but with our eyes as well.

Slides

There are many ways to make the Word of God visible to us and a home mass is a particularly appropriate place to do this. One possibility is using slides for the Liturgy of the Word. Slides of your own family and other members of your parish may be used. They may be sequenced to one of the readings or the responsorial psalm. It is important here that we don't stop to explain each slide but rather let the slides explain the reading. For example if the theme of the mass is reconciliation, we may choose a reading such as the story of the prodigal and then use slides which show how this story might occur in our own lives—a misunderstanding between parents and a teen-age son. Slides may also be used as part of the homily. Again using reconciliation as a theme, we may choose some pictures which show areas in our parish which are in need of reconcili-ation and then have a brief dialogue homily on how we can help to bring about this reconciliation.

Drama

Another way of demonstrating the theme is by drama. Ask a few people to be prepared to act out a brief skit (no more than five minutes) which shows how the theme of the readings is experienced in our lives today. It is important that the accent be kept on our lives today. If we simply try to act out the story as it is written, it comes off false and loses its impact.

Music

Of course music is an important part of the Liturgy of the Word. If there is no song leader among the people who will be coming to the mass, it is possible to use recorded music. Most parish religious education offices have a selection of records to choose from. In using recorded music, it is important that the turning on and off of the music not be a distraction. The person changing the records should be near the turntable and know exactly when to put the music on. Another possibility is to use tapes of music. In this case it is good to lower the volume before turning the machine on or off. This prevents a jarring noise.

Readings

To enrich people's experience of the Liturgy of the Word, it is good to let them know in advance what readings you have chosen for the liturgy. In this way, they may reflect on and pray over them before coming. Of course they should not have the readings in front of them during the Liturgy of the Word. If you are sending written invitations, you might like to include a list of readings and a request that people read them beforehand.

WITH WHOM DO WE CELEBRATE?

When a family celebrates a big event, they naturally think about whom they will invite to this event. Whose presence will help us celebrate? We cannot fully celebrate as individuals. We need others to celebrate with us. So too a family cannot be completely turned in on itself or be self-sufficient. While regular family prayer with just the members of our own family is important, it is not sufficient. We are members of a much larger and richer community than our own families.

To enrich a home mass, it is important to invite a variety of people. The problem usually arises when we try to set limits on who will be invited. Despite the problems it is important to set limits. An easy way to solve the problem is to invite people from a neighborhood, or block or apartment house. Hopefully many families in a parish will have a home mass during the Lenten season and in this way a larger number of parishioners will be able to share in such an experience.

The number of people to be invited is a consideration. The number of people should be in proportion to the space available for the mass. We need to avoid either a "standing room only" atmosphere or a room which echoes because it is so empty. A good norm is to consider how many people can gather comfortably in a semicircle around the table to be used as an altar. There should also be a balance between the number of family members and other invited guests.

ATMOSPHERE

Decorations contribute to (if not create) the festive atmosphere of a party. This is also true of a liturgy. The little extras are very important. In a home mass, we want an atmosphere which is prayerful and reverent on the one hand and comfortable on the other. This atmosphere can be achieved by having everything ready when people arrive. This "everything" includes a table. The table can be any table you have in your home, e.g. a coffee table, a dining room table. Cover the table with a tablecloth. On the table there should be a candle or two, a goblet or pottery cup with wine in it. The cup or goblet should be large enough to hold sufficient wine for everyone. To the side of the table have a small pitcher with water in it. There should also be a plate or basket with bread.

Bread: In order to symbolize more clearly the breaking and sharing of the one bread, the *General Instruction of the Roman Missal* strongly urges that the bread to be used for the Eucharist look and taste like real food. A home mass is an ideal setting for the breaking and sharing of the bread. Small loaves of unleavened bread such as the Greek or Syrian breads are available in frozen food departments of grocery stores. You may wish to make your own bread or ask one of the invited guests to bring the bread. A recipe for Eucharistic bread follows this article.

It most probably will not be necessry for you to provide anything else for the altar. It would be good to check with the priest and ask him to bring anything else he feels he needs.

You may wish to add some decoration to the table such as flowers. If you do add something, it should be simple and not dominate the table. The bread and wine should be the focal point of the table.

If at all possible, avoid using strong overhead lighting. The use of lamps and candlelight greatly enhances a reflective atmosphere.

Be sure that the readers are prepared beforehand and that each reader has copy of the reading so that the Liturgy of the Word will flow smoothly.

If there is going to be singing, it is good to practice the songs briefly before beginning the mass. Also allow time for introductions and greetings before beginning. Be sure that everybody has at least met everybody else. The extra time and effort that this takes greatly contributes to a community atmosphere.

Refreshment

Following the liturgy, it is good to have some type of refreshment. Depending on the time of the liturgy, you may wish to have a pot luck supper or coffee and cake. The invited guests should know beforehand what to expect in this regard. Whatever form of refreshment you decide to have, ask people to bring something for this. This action says that you really want these people to be part of the community because you are asking them to make a contribution to the community.

After all of the planning, the only thing left for you and your family to do is to enjoy the prayerful experience of a worshipping community.

The following is a brief check list to aid in your planning. You may find it helpful to go through this with the priest who will be celebrating the liturgy.

HOME MASS CHECK LIST
Home Mass

Place _____

Date _____

Celebrant _____

Theme _____

Readings and Readers: _____

_____

_____

Liturgy of the Word

Slides _____

Drama _____

Other _____

Music or Records

_____

_____

Materials Required

Table _____ Bread _____

Table cloth _____ Cup _____

Candle(s) _____ Plate _____

Wine _____

Books for Readings _____

Copies of Music _____

_____

Invited Guests

_____

_____

_____

Follow-up Rrefreshments

_____

_____

_____

Recipe For Eucharistic Bread

MATZO BREAD

Ingredients:
2/3 cup boiling water
1/3 cup oil (vegetable or peanut)
1 tablespoon sugar
1/2 teaspoon salt
1 1/2 cups matzoh meal
3 eggs

Directions:
Mix together first four ingredients. Add matzoh meal. Add eggs one at a time, beating well after each egg is added. Wet hands with cold water to keep from sticking to dough. Roll dough into circles about 4 or 5 inches in diameter.

Bake on greased cookie sheets at 400° for about thirty minutes or until golden brown.

Yield: 5-7 small loaves, each loaf serving 8-10 people.

THE SEDER MEAL AS A CHRISTIAN HOME CELEBRATION
Gerald Twomey, C.S.P.

Introduction

Passover is the great Jewish feast of redemption and liberation, the memorial of the Israelites' deliverance from their bondage in Egypt. The word Passover means "deliverance," since in the story of the Exodus Yahweh "passed over the houses of the children of Israel in Egypt" (Ex. 12:27). Passover is also known as the Feast of Unleavened Bread, since in their haste to flee Egypt, "the people carried off their dough, still unleavened" (Ex. 12:34). The lamb offered at each paschal meal recalls the first Passover sacrifice, whose blood protected the Israelites from the avenging angel of Yahweh (cf. Ex. 12:21-33). Passover is a festival of great rejoicing, which reveals how God "led us from captivity to freedom, from sadness to joy, from mourning to feasting, from servitude to redemption, from darkness to brilliant light."

The Seder Meal

The ritual meal which commemorates the events of the Exodus is called the Seder.

The primary aim of the Seder is to transmit to future generations the story of the Exodus, the central event in Jewish history. Ideally, a family gathers around a table in its own home to celebrate the Seder, sharing in a meal which symbolizes their consciousness as a people and their faith in the future. The Exodus story pertains to all persons, since it tells of the right of all persons to be free.

Celebrating Our Heritage

In the Christian tradition the Passover Seder is also believed to be when Jesus instituted the Eucharist. Gathered around the supper table with his disciples, Jesus told them, "I have longed to eat this Passover with you before I suffer; because, I tell you, I shall not eat it again until it is fulfilled in the kingdom of God.

Then, taking a cup, he gave thanks and said, 'Take this and share it among you, because from now on, I tell you, I shall not drink wine until the kingdom of God comes'.

Then he took some bread, and when he had given thanks, broke it and gave it to them, saying, 'This is my body which will be given for you; do this as a memorial of me'. He did the same with the cup after supper, and said, 'This cup is the new covenant in my blood which will be poured out for you.' " (Luke 22:15-20)

This Christian observance of this ritual meal celebrates not only our tradition of Christ's last supper but our own Jewish heritage which provided the context for Jesus' institution at the last supper.

Elements of the Seder

The Seder meal is accompanied by commentary, prayers and, where possible, songs. Since the Seder is a commemoration of the Exodus story, it is strongly recommended that prior to the celebration all participants read and reflect on the scripture account of this event which is found in chapters seven through thirteen of the book of Exodus. This account serves as an excellent family Lenten reading program, and reflection on it will greatly enhance the celebration of the Seder.

The actual celebration of the Seder is a complete meal with supper during the ritual. In the service which follows, the meal is a ritual or symbolic one and supper follows the ritual. Like the Seder, it should be festive and joyous. If there are invited guests coming to the Seder, they could each be asked to bring something for the supper. This increases the feeling of harmony and community.

Before the celebration set the table as for a dinner.

Each plate should have small portions of the following:

HAROSET:

combine ½ chopped nuts

½ diced apple

1 T. cinnamon

1 T. sugar

Red wine as desired

This recipe can be increased to serve any number; it should serve 4 to 6 people.

MARROR:

a bitter herb such as the top of the horseradish root or parsley

EGG: one slice of hard cooked egg

SALT WATER: a separate small dish next to the dinner plate.

WINE GLASS: This should be empty at the beginning of the meal.

MATZAH: one piece.

In addition to these items, the leader should have:

THREE MATZOT: one on top of the other

MATZAH RECIPE

You may use an ordinary biscuit dough recipe and delete the baking soda and baking powder or use the following:

Mix well: 3¼ cups flour

1 cup water

1 T. salt

Divide into three equal balls of dough. Shape each into a very thin circle 6 to 8 in. diameter.

Place on a greased cookie sheet and prick the dough with a fork. Bake in a preheated oven at 500° for 5-6 min. or until brown.

RED WINE: A Carafe or pitcher with sufficient wine for each person to participate in three cups.

NAPKIN: A separate plate with a napkin on it. This will be used to cover the afikoman (hidden portion) during the meal.

LAMB: A plate with a small piece of lamb for each person. This can easily be done by cooking a few lamb chops and cutting them into a sufficient number of pieces.

Music Makes A Difference

Music greatly adds to the celebration of the Seder, particularly if it can be sung by those present. If the group lacks talented musicians or vocalists, recorded music can be used. It is especially appropriate to sing the Psalms included in the service, or at least antiphons suited to them. (*The Psalms: A New Translation/Singing Version.* New York: Paulist Press, 1968.)

This service provides for an opening and closing song. Use only suitable songs you know or the ones listed here.

"We Long For You, O Lord" (FEL)
"God and Man at Table are Sat Down" (Word of Life)
"Of My Hands" (FEL)
"Sabbath Prayer" (From Fiddler On The Roof)
"Take Our Bread" (WLSM)
"Go Down Moses" (Negro Spiritual)
"Song of Moses" (Word of Life)
"Keep In Mind" (WLSM)
"Where Charity and Love Prevail" (WLSM)
"Look Beyond" (FEL)
"Peace I Leave With You, My Friends" (FEL)

Roles to be Performed

Apart from its religious basis, the most important ingredients of the Seder are good company and good food. While the company should center on the family present, it achieves a fuller flavor if some guests participate.

Ideally, the role of LEADER is filled by a parent.

One of the participants should be designated as SERVER.

Often a guest is asked to assume a role such as COMMENTATOR.

Usually a woman (preferably the mother) begins the service by lighting the festive candles.

Those parts labelled PARTICIPANT can be filled by older children of the household.

Traditionally the "four questions" are posed by the YOUNGEST person present. Everyone is encouraged to participate fully in the meal, in prayer, conversation and music.

Further Remarks

Modification of the Seder: This service may be freely adapted or simplified, but it seeks to preserve much of the richness of the Jewish ritual meal presented in a Christian context. It is recommended that the essential elements remain intact, to retain the full flavor and rich symbolism which the Seder holds for all believers.

A Leisurely Meal: The participants should relax and enjoy the events of the Seder. American society has lost the sense of meal as ritual, as a time of thanksgiving or commemoration. The participants should be encouraged to enjoy and savor the company, the ceremony, the food, and the song which bring life to the Seder meal.

Table decorations should be simple and tasteful. They should include festive candles, a tablecloth, and where possible, flowers.

Seder As Liturgy: The service should be experienced as a para-liturgy, but is easily adaptable to a liturgy of the Eucharist, especially a home Mass. Ideally it is enacted on the night of the Jewish Passover, or prior to the evening liturgy on Holy Thursday. Any Lenten evening would be suitably appropriate, but the closer to the events of Holy Week, the better.

When we observe the Passover meal as a Christian home celebration, our understanding of important New Testament truths is enriched. We recognize more fully God's active role in human affairs and indeed his presence in our own lives. Within the context of this ritual meal our sense of presence to one another as family and friends is deepened. Our appreciation of the sacrament of the Eucharist is heightened. We discover the firm spiritual roots which our faith has in Judaism, and realize more fully the bonds which join us to our Jewish brothers and sisters.

The Seder meal can serve as a moving and deeply spiritual experience for us all. It spurs us on: "to life! . . . to freedom! . . . to Jerusalem!"

THE SEDER MEAL
(Adapted celebration based on the Passover Meal)

SANCTIFICATION OF THE FESTIVAL
Commentator: The central theme of the Passover is redemption. For us Passover means not only the physical exodus from Egypt, but our spiritual passing over from the bondage of sin as well. The aim of the Seder on this night of the Passover is to bring the events and miracles of the past deliverance from Egypt into the present, so that each of us gathered here feels as though we had personally come out of bondage. We are asked to bear witness to God's redeeming action in the past, to act in conformity with his will in the present, and to renew our hope in further redemption.

KADESH, SANCTIFICATION OF THE DAY
Leader: We gather for this sacred celebration in the presence of loved ones and friends with the signs of festive rejoicing around us. Together with the whole house of Israel, both young and old are linking the past with future; we respond in faith to God's call to service; we gather here to observe the Passover, as it is written:

All: "The feast of unleavened bread must be kept, because it was on that same day I brought your armies out of the land of Egypt. Keep that day from age to age . . ." (Ex. 12:17)

Opening Song: (see Introduction for an appropriate song which can be used here.)

LIGHTING OF THE FESTIVE CANDLES

Woman present: In praising God we say that all life is sacred. In kindling these festive lights, we are reminded of life's sanctity. With every holy candle we light, the world is brightened to a higher harmony. We praise you, O Lord our God, King of the Universe who hallow our lives with commandments and bid us to light these festive holy lights. *(She lights the Festive Candles.)*

THE KIDDUSH, THE FIRST CUP

Commentator: We have blessed this day in the *Kadesh,* and called to mind the holiness of this festival commanded by the Lord. The candles we have lighted praise God for the holiness of all life.

Now let us prepare to drink the first, the Kiddush, or cup of sanctification. Traditionally, four times during the meal wine is taken, recalling the four terms in the Exodus story which describe God's action in rescuing the Israelites: "I brought out . . . I saved . . . I delivered . . . I redeemed." We bless the wine and every food which is eaten, and every action which takes place, as a gesture of thanksgiving to the Creator of all things. *(The Leader pours wine for all.)*

Leader: Our history teaches us that in varied ways and in different words God gave promises of freedom to our people. With cups of wine we recall each one of them, as now the first:

All: 'I am Yahweh. *I will free you* from the burdens which the Egyptians lay on you." (Ex. 6:6)

Leader: (*All raise wine glasses*) We raise the Kiddush cup, and proclaim the holiness of the Day of Deliverance.
All: Blessed are you, O Lord our God, King of the Universe, who have kept us in life, sustained us, and brought us to this session of joy! (*All drink the first cup.*)

KARPAS—REBIRTH AND RENEWAL
Commentator: In the springtime each year, the season of rebirth and renewal, we read from the Song of Songs. This poetry of nature and of love recalls for us the love between God and the people of Israel, and their covenant relationship. The parsley (or other green herb) symbolizes the growth of springtime, and is a sign of hope and renewal.
Leader: "See, winter is past, the rains are over and gone. The flowers appear on the earth. The season of glad songs has come . . ." (Song 2:10-12). (*Each person takes some greens and dips them twice in salt water.*)
All: Blessed are you, O Lord our God, King of the Universe, Creator of the fruit of the earth! (*The greens are now eaten.*)

YAHATZ—A BOND FORMED BY SHARING
Commentator: The leader breaks the middle matzah on his plate, wraps the larger half in a cloth, and conceals it as the *afikoman*. This matzah is later shared as the final food of the Seder, but now serves as a visible reminder of the hidden Messiah whose appearance is expectantly awaited.
Leader: (*While breaking the middle matzah*) This is the bread of affliction, the poor bread which our ancestors ate in the land of Egypt. Let all who are hungry come and eat. Let all who are in want share in the hope of Passover. As we celebrate here, we join with people everywhere. This year we celebrate here. Next year in the land of Israel. Now we are still enslaved. Next year may we all be free.

MATZAH, MAROR, HAROSET

(The first of the leader's three matzot is broken and distributed.)

All: Blessed are you, O Lord our God, King of the Universe, who bring forth bread from the earth. We praise you, who hallow our lives with commandments, and have commanded us regarding the eating of matzah and maror.

Commentator: Matzah is used to recall the fact that the dough used by the fleeing Israelites had no time to rise before the act of redemption.

Maror, the top of the horseradish root, symbolizes the bitterness of the past suffering of the Jews in Egypt.

Haroset is a mixture of apples, spices, wine and nuts, and symbolizes the mortar the Jews used in carrying out the Pharoah's labor.

According to ancient custom, maror and haroset are eaten between two pieces of matzot. Break the piece of matzah on your plate in half and place some maror and haroset between.

All: In each of these elements we see the symbols of our story: the matzah of freedom, the maror of slavery, the haroset of toil. For in the time of bondage there is hope of redemption, and in the time of freedom, there is knowledge of servitude. *(All eat the matzah, maror, and haroset.)*

THE FOUR QUESTIONS

The youngest person now asks the four traditional questions, which serve as an introduction to the Scripture. The questions are asked by the youngest, because each generation is obligated to make the Exodus its own, and because the parent is obligated by Scripture to recount for his or her children what the Lord has done for them.

Youngest present: Why does this night differ from all other nights? On all other nights we eat leavened bread; why on this night only matzah? On all other nights we eat all kinds of herbs; why on this night only bitter herbs? On all other nights we do not dip our herbs at all; why on this night must we dip them twice? On all other nights we eat in an ordinary manner; why on this night do we dine with special ceremony?

MAGGID—THE NARRATION

Leader: There are many questions to answer. Now we begin to respond to them. Our history moves from slavery toward freedom.

All: We were slaves to Pharaoh in Egypt, and the Lord freed us with a mighty hand. Had the Lord not delivered us from Egypt, we, our children, and children's children would still be enslaved.

Leader: Therefore, even if all of us were wise, if all of us were a people of understanding, and learned in the law and the prophets, it would still be our obligation to retell the story of the Exodus from Egypt. Anyone who searches deeply into its meaning is considered praiseworthy.

All: Our redemption is not yet complete.

Leader: (As the leader lifts the paschal lamb, he or she asks . . .) What is the meaning of the pasch?

Participant: This pasch represents the paschal lamb which our ancestors sacrificed to the Lord in memory of the night on which the Holy One passed over the houses of our ancestors in Egypt. As it is written: "And when your children ask you, 'What does this ritual mean?' you will tell them, 'It is the sacrifice of the Passover in honor of Yahweh who passed over the houses of the sons and daughters of Israel in Egypt, but spared our houses!' " (Ex. 12:26-27). *(The leader holds up the upper piece of unleavened bread.)*

Leader: What is the meaning of the unleavened bread?

Participant: It is the bread of affliction, which our ancestors took with them out of Egypt. For, as it is written: "They baked cakes with the dough which they had brought from Egypt, unleavened because they had been driven out of Egypt with no time for dallying, and had not provided themselves with food for the journey." (Ex. 12:39) *(The leader replaces the matzah, and holds up the bitter herbs.)*

Leader: What is the meaning of the maror?

Participant: Maror means bitter herb, and symbolizes the bitterness of past suffering which our ancestors experienced in Egypt. As it is written, "The Egyptians forced the children of Israel into slavery, and made their lives unbearable with hard labor, work with clay and with brick, all kinds of work in the fields; they forced on them every kind of labor." (Ex. 1:13-14)

Commentator: This part of the service ends with the prayers of thanksgiving to God through chanting one of the Psalms of deliverance, and drinking the second cup of wine, the cup of deliverance.

(All together recite or sing Psalm 114.)

PSALM 114   Hymn for the Passover
Alleluia!

When Israel came out of Egypt,
the House of Jacob from a foreign nation,
Judah became his sanctuary
and Israel his domain.

The sea fled at the sight,
the Jordan stopped flowing,
the mountains skipped like rams,
and like lambs, the hills.

Sea, what makes you run away?
Jordan, why stop flowing?

Why skip like rams, you mountains,
why like lambs, you hills?

Quake, earth, at the coming of your Master,
at the coming of the God of Jacob,
who turns rock into pool
flint into fountain.

Leader: With the second cup of wine, we recall the second promise of liberation.

All: *"I will deliver you."* (Ex. 6:6)

Leader: It is written: "And on that day you shall explain to your children, 'This is because of what Yahweh did for me when I came out of Egypt.' " It is not only our ancestors that the Lord redeemed, but he redeemed us as well along with them, and all generations to come. *(The participants raise their cups and say:)*

All: Therefore, we are bound to thank, praise, honor, bless and adore him who brought us forth from slavery to freedom, from sorrow to joy, from mourning to feasting, from bondage to redemption, from darkness to great light. We praise you, O God, King of the Universe, Creator of the fruit of the vine! *(All drink the second cup. The symbolic meal is now served.)*

Commentator: The meal is customarily begun with hard-boiled eggs flavored with salt water. The egg is symbolic of new growth, new hope, new life. *(Each person dips a slice of egg in salt water and eats it.)*

Commentator: The meat is eaten according to the custom that: "The flesh (of the lamb) is to be eaten, roasted over fire; it must be eaten with unleavened bread and bitter herbs." (Exodus 12:8). *(The server now gives each person a symbolic piece of lamb [or other meat] which is eaten.)*

Commentator: We believe that at this point in the Lord's Supper Jesus instituted the Eucharist. We read in Luke's Gospel: "He took bread, and when he had given thanks, broke it and gave it to them saying, 'This is my body, which will be given for you; do this as a memorial of me.' " (Lk. 22:19)

Leader: As we now share the bread of the afikoman, let us realize that the fellowship which binds us together is the grace and peace we share as members of the Body of Christ. (*All eat of the afikoman.*)

Commentator: Luke's account continues: "He did the same with the cup after supper, and said, 'This cup is the New Covenant in my blood which will be poured out for you'" (Lk. 22:20). Here we clearly see the connection between the cup of Jesus' New Covenant and our final cup of the Seder, the cup of redemption. (*Wine is poured for each person.*)

Leader: Let us together take up our cups of wine, and recall the final promise:

All: As it is written: "*I will redeem you* with an outstretched arm." Praised are you, O Lord our God, King of the Universe, Creator of the fruit of the vine! (*All drink the final cup of wine.*)

GESTURE OF PEACE

Leader: We have now celebrated our unity in this symbolic meal, in sharing this bread and this wine. We recall the words of the Lord Jesus at this point in the Last Supper: "Peace I leave you, my own peace I give you, a peace the world cannot give . . ."

Let us now offer one another an appropriate sign of the peace we have experienced here as the company of believers gathered to celebrate these mysteries of our faith. (*All exchange a sign of peace.*)

Leader: Let us conclude our ritual by joining our hands and hearts in praying the words which Jesus offered to his Father for us on the night we recall here.

All: Holy Father, keep those you have given me true to your name, so that they may be one as we are one . . .

I am not asking you to remove them from the world, but to protect them from the Evil One . . .

Consecrate them in truth—your word is truth. As you sent

me into the world, I have sent them into the world . . .

May they all be one. Father, may they be one in us, as you are in me and I am in you, so that the world may believe it was you who sent me. (*Pause for silent prayer.*)

FINAL BLESSING
Leader: Let us bless each other.
All: May the Lord bless us and keep us!
May the Lord let his face shine
   upon us and be gracious to us!
May the Lord look upon us kindly,
   and grant us peace!
Amen!

Closing Song: (see *Introduction for suggestions*).

The complete meal is now served in a spirit of festivity and celebration. In the Hebrew tradition it is actually incorporated into the preceding ritual meal.

As we enjoy this meal, let us remember that Jesus became the fulfillment of all the promises of redemption and deliverance we mark here tonight. Jesus has called us out of darkness and made us his chosen people of the New Covenant. That is why we gather here tonight. That is why we celebrate this meal. Jesus, the Lamb of God, has offered himself for the forgiveness of our sins. Happy are we who share in this supper.

ADDITIONAL RESOURCES
The Paschal Meal (Grailville, Ohio: The Grail, 1965).
The Passover Meal: A Ritual for Christian Homes (New York: Paulist Press, 1972).
The Passover Haggadah (New York: Schocken Books, 1969).
It's The Lord's Supper: Eucharist of Christians (New York: Paulist Press, 1976).
A Feast of History (New York: Simon and Schuster, 1972).
The Eucharist Today (New York: Paulist Press, 1968).

LIFE IN LIFE
Adult Discussion Series

PRAYER AND SPIRITUAL GROWTH

PRAYER AND SPIRITUAL GROWTH   SESSION 1

ESSAY: **REND OUR HEARTS**

Words can lose their homes and lack their original meanings. "Rend your hearts, not your garments, return to the Lord, your God." (Joel 2:13) What can that mean: "rend your hearts"?

Last summer I drove up 14th Street in Washington, D.C., where innumerable hookers were out soliciting. Adult movies and massage parlors were available for the price stipulated. Men were pouring tar along a sidewalk and an older woman was pushing a wire grocery cart with one bag of groceries in it.

On many of the buildings were pasted posters of Reverend Sun Moon with his invitation to repent and to join his Unification Church. As I drove farther I finally arrived in a suburb to meet a friend at the neighborhood swimming pool. I sank into a chair to listen to a group of women behind me discussing very nervously the nervous problems of an absent friend. The contrast within one hour was too obvious for my mind to be at ease with it.

Could I assume that the hookers ought to rend their hearts? It would be a *moral* conversion perhaps. Should I want the women at the pool to talk with greater depth? It would have been a welcome *intellectual* conversion if they had. Ought I to expect that if one followed Sun Moon (s)he had had a *religious* conversion?

The book of Genesis tells us that we are created in the image of God. It also tells us that we are capable of great selfishness when it comes to choice of pleasure and pain. Our hearts learn good and evil patterns of relating to reality. What can "rending our hearts" mean *concretely*? Obviously, it must somehow mean being in the process of moral, intellectual and religious conversions all our lives. But surely God cannot ask us "to tear apart, to divide" (Webster's Dictionary!) our hearts?

The key to understanding conversion, our own, may be in the second part of the verse: ". . . return to me with your whole heart." Return to the person each of us is and is becoming may feel like a great rending—a painful splitting-up of the false securities and divisive patterns which paralyze our energies to truly love. Returning to God is likely to be returning to ourselves.

QUESTIONS FOR REFLECTION

1. Have there been times when I wished others would change their ways and yet I did not wish to change my behavior?
2. Have I ever felt conversion as a change of behavior? What was it like?

3. At certain times have I experienced changes in my life's meaning? Birth of a child, death of a loved one, a failure which caused depression or a success which brought joy?
4. Why do some people seem to live as if they need to change nothing in their lives?
5. Do I generally experience turning to God as a sudden thing or a gradual development which comes out of life circumstances?
6. What do I need to change in order to turn to the Lord?

SCRIPTURE READING Cycle A, B, C *(Joel 2:12-18)*

My resolution: _____

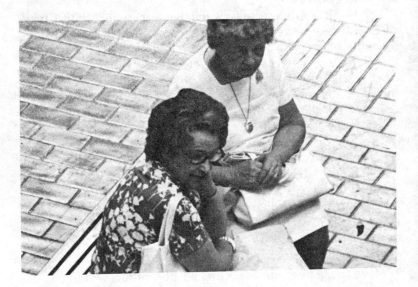

PRAYER AND SPIRITUAL GROWTH *SESSION 2*
ESSAY: **GRACE IS IN RELATIONSHIPS**

Some months ago I spent a weekend retreating with friends in a West Virginia cabin. We drank margueritas, sang songs, walked in the woods and tried to find out by phone if Boston was winning or losing its ballgame. One afternoon when I was walking with a friend I asked a question which had been on my mind, in my heart, for some time, "What do you think grace is?"

My friend answered, "I think that it is in relationships." I was startled in such a way perhaps that a person would be who asks "What is a house?" when he/she is standing inside one.

To say that grace is in relationships does not reduce grace to a new psychological process. The principles of the science do indeed help us to understand grace better but we are talking about much more here. Very often in the Lenten liturgical readings, we hear about relationships. The readings speak of a covenant being made and of the establishment of a relationship between God and humanity and between people and people. The Lord offers us a relationship with himself. The relationship is offered by a loving God, a caring God who created us and gave us life and who continues to care for us when we throw that life out of proportion. This grace/relationship involves a God who is concerned for and with us and so we are to be as he is—concerned and caring for others. Often we think of grace as a commodity purchased from the heavenly upstairs storehouse. Although this notion of grace is hardly adequate, it is at times easier to think in terms of something we accomplish rather than in terms of something that is offered to us because we are loved.

In Jesus we see much of grace. He went about inviting relationships. He gathered around him people who accepted this relationship with himself that he offered. These people also entered into a relationship with one another. The relationship gradually deepened and they became a community of believers.

Jesus sent his Spirit to strengthen those relationships when they were in danger of dissipation through fear. His sending his Spirit tells us something about the type of relationship he offered. He did not offer a casual, cozy type of relating which one could take up when it felt good and put down when it didn't. His whole life tells us that relating to others could be the most costly venture of human life. His acceptance of his own death tells us that he considered such a venture worth the risk even if it ended as his seemed to. He gave up life—his own life for the sake of our relationship to the Father. He understood that life's hardest moments are often life-giving events. He knew that life's darkest moments are often laden with joy and hope. Jesus worked through his relationship to us and to his Father to the end. In working through a relationship, there comes a unique strength. Out of this comes life.

Obviously grace is not the same as transactional analysis nor parent effectiveness skills. It can perhaps be mediated wherever this kind of sharing in love and in truth happen. In fact, many of today's psychological skills may remind us of the fact that we block grace by selfishness, by not being faithful to the truths we feel about ourselves and by our failure to trust.

Grace is in relating to God and to others and in celebrating that relationship. That does not necessarily mean that if we fail in relationships we fail in grace. Part of grace may well be to learn which relationships we can enter and those which must fail. We must learn to discern those relationships which are life giving, which are graceful.

It is good to reflect often on how grace is present in our lives. Who are the people who mediate grace for me? Who are the people who strengthen my relationship with the Lord?

QUESTIONS FOR REFLECTION

1. When someone uses the word "grace" what is the first thought I have? Does it seem far removed from my life ex-

periences of every day or very near to me?

2. Do I see grace as coming from outside and above the earth, a pipeline from eternity?
3. Can I locate a moment when I, indeed, *felt* grace?
4. What relationships that I have, imperfect and in process as they may be, seem to be a grace, a gift?

SCRIPTURE READING Cycle A (*Genesis 2:7-9; 3:1-7*)
Cycle B (*Genesis 9:8-15*) Cycle C (*Deuteronomy 26:4-10*)
My resolution:

PRAYER AND SPIRITUAL GROWTH SESSION 3
ESSAY: **PROMISES, PROMISES**
Not long ago I sat at a rally listening to promises being made and criticisms being hurled. Speaker after speaker promised "better things," and ways out of present difficulty in the justice

system. Hundreds of people sat before the onslaught of words looking very bored and very passive. *Promises, promises.*

We can turn on stereo any hour of the day or night to hear love songs of promises kept or promises which were never really intended to be kept. We can hear anytime the promise from politicians that government will support legislation for our pet hopes as well as our great human social needs.

All of us have suffered to one degree or another the promise of a friendship which was withdrawn when hard days came for us. We have known friends who stayed with us. We have sometimes moved out to friends in their time of need and sometimes we have broken a promise and not reached out.

Banks promise full security. Condominium realtors promise idyllic surroundings. Cosmetic ads promise beauty. Sooner or later we weary of so many unkept promises and ask what does a promise really mean. What may be lacking in most promise-making is a process to get to the reward. The process towards a loving relationship is arduous, full of great joy and harsh moments of communication. The process towards our own growth may mean giving up our limited notions and expectations of others. It may mean believing promises which seem impossible of fulfillment. The process towards a promise of justice is fought with hard, concrete labor, lobbying and individual responsibility.

God promised Abraham a posterity, a new people. He apparently trusted the process to God and acted: Reading the first few chapters of Genesis we see what means God took to lead his friend, Abraham. The promised land was far and required a very strenuous journey. It did not come as a first gift, full security in the beginning. It came after struggle, loss and doubt. The history of God's people is a continual recalling of how God really did keep a promise. In times of greatest suffering his people remembered what once he had done for Abraham. We might ask ourselves if we really believe that God will keep his promises in regard to our lives or if God seems a kind but disinterested figure off in the heavens acting like a control-tower expert.

The story of Abraham is a story of a man learning who God is. This God of Abraham is not like other gods. He keeps his promises; he is faithful; he cares for his people; he does not require human sacrifice. Abraham spent his whole life giving up his limited notion of God. Our own spiritual growth requires that we do this too. We have to give up our pet ideas about God in order to learn more and more who he is.

We might ask ourselves whether or not we fully accept Jesus' promise of fullness of life. Do we consider this a nice idea that will never be a reality? Or do we really believe that God can take our lives and make them full and rich ones?

QUESTIONS FOR REFLECTION
1. Can I recall a time a promise was made to me and not kept? How did I feel: sad, angry, cynical?
2. Can I recall a time a promise was fulfilled beyond my expectations? How did I feel then: happy, secure, amazed?
3. Do I sometimes stifle the growth of others by my limited expectations of them?
4. What are my expectations of God?
5. What limited ideas of God do I have to give up in order to know him better?

SCRIPTURE READING

Cycle A   (Genesis 12:1-4a)

Cycle B   (Genesis 22:1-2, 9, 10-13, 15-18)

Cycle C   (Genesis 15:5-12, 17-18)

My resolution: _____

_____

_____

PRAYER AND SPIRITUAL GROWTH   SESSION 4
ESSAY: **GOD: NEAR-IN OR FAR-OUT?**

Prayer opens us to the mystery of God. We meet our own limitations as we approach him. Yet also we find him in the events which are very near to us. The poet Rainer Maria Rilke wrote of prayer as going outside of self to God visible in the universe:

> I would like to walk
> out of my heart
> under the wide sky.
> I would like to pray.

Lament

David Burrell, a contemporary philosopher, speaks of the search to find God within one's experience:

> "It is . . . that in surrendering myself to the shape of my life, to my destiny, I am led into God himself. Or to speak more modestly, I am brought to a point where I may cele-

brate the fact that I belong to him—a no-place beyond the parameters of self where my soul can magnify the Lord. The language of 'belonging' is another useful indicator that we are speaking not of self but of soul. For one person cannot justly belong to another. Yet at that point whence I receive my life, I can justly and joyfully belong to the source of that life. At that same point, prayer ceases to be an encounter or a conversation, and becomes a joyful surrender and receiving oneself as gift.'' *Prayer as the Language of the Soul* (David Burrell, *Soundings,* Winter, 1971)

The nearness or distance of God was always a question which Moses faced. His people demanded of him, "Is the Lord in our midst or not?" (Ex 17:7) Yet Moses' own experience of God was marked by awareness of his distance and his otherness. Moses took off his shoes (Ex 3:5) before a God who uttered commands which he wished kept. (Ex 20:1-17)

Often when we see the world of nature in a sight like the Grand Canyon or from a Rocky Mountain cabin, God seems near. He seems near in times of security and joy and peace. We welcome his presence in our midst as we celebrate the Eucharist. But God may seem far away in sorrow; he may seem to have hidden his face at the sight of our suffering. Elie Wiesel, the great Jewish writer, writes of his experience of the absence of God as he sees the smoke of the concentration camp and knows that this smoke is from his relatives' bodies.

Yet God may seem far away in the sense of his majesty and his holiness, also. Whatever we know of him we also know that our understanding does not do justice to who God is. He is LORD. We pray to this God who seems like the moon to have two faces. We may wake up at night and know that all is well for God is our friend. We spend periods of time away from friends or family. We wonder why God seems far away in the absence of a loved one. This is not to suggest that God is a split reality. It is not to suggest that there is a right or a wrong way to pray and to sense his presence. It is not a case of needing one or the other approach to him. It is a case of God's being present within the reality of our everyday lives and also being so much more than our lives.

QUESTIONS FOR REFLECTION
1. When in my life do I sense God as near to me?
2. When in my life do I sense God as far from me, beyond me because of his goodness and power?
3. When do I find myself wondering where he is and if he cares for me at all?
4. Are there experiences of my everyday life in which I know God is present?

SCRIPTURE READING
Cycle A   (Exodus 17:3-7)
Cycle B   (Exodus 20:1-3, 7-8, 12-17)
Cycle C   (Exodus 3:1-8a, 13-15)
My resolution: _____

PRAYER AND SPIRITUAL GROWTH   SESSION 5
ESSAY: **PRAYER: CHANGING GOD OR US?**
Prayer does not function as a kind of behavioral modification of God. Its intent is really not to change God's intent toward us. From what we know of God from Scripture he does not have a capricious plan that we must try to persuade him not to execute. Neither does he stand aloof from our lives as some would wish us to believe. It is true that sometimes he does seem far away. But it seems clear from Scripture that God wants our goodness and our acceptance of life. He wants what is our good.

Often we hear that prayer changes us. That may be partially true. We can all recall events in our lives when we learned from prayer a new way to relate to some reality in our lives. The poet Richard Hanley put it this way:

"Lord make me an instrument
    Of thy peace"—
This I sang (ignorant
Of "instrument"),
And grew so utterly resigned
So strangely warm
And weak, as when running wanly
Through the guilt of dreams.
from *Prelude to Liturgy*

Yet basically if prayer is a personal meeting of man with God its intent is not change. Its intent is simply what it is: loving or worried exchange with a God who has told us that he cares. Have you ever had a friend who always wishes to change you? Conversation with such a friend gets tedious and becomes a torment. With friends we need to be accepted. We need to grow, to be invited into the best that we are and the better that we can become. Prayer allows us to accept acceptance and simply be as we are: sinner, saint and the many layers in between both. Today's reading reminds us that it is acceptable to let God know that we experience darkness and lack of sight and a sense of being lost. How we pray depends so much upon how we view God.

QUESTIONS FOR REFLECTION
1. Do I have the idea that when I pray I change God's mind?
2. When I converse with others do I have it on my mind how much they need to change?
3. Have I ever prayed and simply felt accepted and wished nothing to be changed?
4. Isn't it also realistic to believe that God will help to change things in my life which need change?
5. What do I think Psalm 108 means when it states, "But I, I am Prayer"?

SCRIPTURE READING

Cycle A   (John 9:1-41)

Cycle B   (John 3:14-21)

Cycle C   (Luke 15:1-3, 11-32)

My resolution: _____

_____

_____

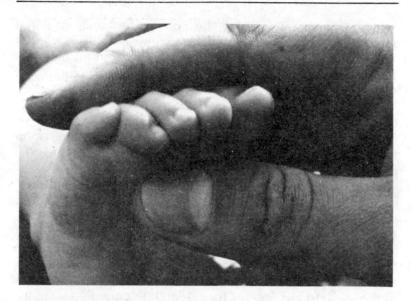

PRAYER AND SPIRITUAL GROWTH   SESSION 6
ESSAY: **COUNT ON US**

The Super Giant grocery chain has a musical ad which goes, "We've got the spirit; count on us."

That was the constant utterance of the early church. They said it a good deal in their actions more than in their words. The letter to the Philippians tells us: "I wish to know Christ and the power flowing from his resurrection. . . ." (3:10) The spirit versus flesh struggle which Romans 8:8-11 describes is seen resolved in the power of Christ's victory. Yet the book of Hebrews reminds us that power was given Jesus because of his obedience. (5:7-9)

Not long ago I lived through the death of my favorite aunt. My 85-year-old uncle was left alone by the death. They had had no children. At the time my uncle seemed to be holding to life by the narrow thread of hope that said, "I can count on you, my family." Of course, he could. The family gathered forces to find care. I wondered at the time and still do wonder how many people look to the family of God in his believers and count on them. Is the strong statement from Super Giant true of the local parish?

"We've got the Spirit; COUNT ON US." That is a way of saying what Jesus meant by beatitude. The church promises by the fact of its being given his Spirit that it can be counted upon for support, care and concern when there is need. That is the promise of the church.

Yet the church is of many members. Some keep beatitudes; others of us do not always live up to their meanings. Most of us could not be counted upon to do what Mother Teresa of Calcutta does: taking the dying off the streets of India and giving their death a last concerned dignity. But we can be counted upon to alleviate what Margaret Mead calls the American illness of loneliness. We can be counted upon to bring meals to the aged, to give money for research to cure disease, to listen to those who need to be listened to (which is all of us).

Sometimes it is not easy to be counted upon. It can get in the way of a fast trip home from the office if we see a stranded traveler. It can be a real bore to listen when the person has told the story for the twentieth time the same way. It can be inconvenient to stop a good novel to hear a child tell how she was called a name she did not like.

The Spirit Jesus promised makes us accountable for each other. People count on us; we count on them. Psychology calls such action "interrelatedness"; theology might name it "community." Whatever its name, its face is love.

QUESTIONS FOR REFLECTION
1. When have I felt drained and tired and turned to another upon whom I could count? Have I ever associated such power to help and heal with the Spirit of Jesus?

2. Do I look to the church for strength and energy in time of distress? To the large church, the local parish or fellow Christians?

3. Do I know people whom I could count on no matter what happened to me? Do I realize that others who help me and seem strong also need me to support them? Pastors, parish helpers, family strongholds?

4. The spirit of Jesus helps us to live with a kind of power that comes of mutual support. How and in whom do I see the strength of gospel life being lived?

5. How can others count on me?

SCRIPTURE READING   *Cycle A*   *(Romans 8:8-11)*
Cycle B   *(Hebrews 5:7-9)*   *Cycle C*   *(Phil. 3:8-14)*

My resolution: _____

PRAYER AND SPIRITUAL GROWTH   SESSION 7
ESSAY: **PASSION, PAIN AND PLEASURE**

Many of us embrace pleasure with very spontaneous hearts. Can we even imagine someone saying, "I have to dance this Polish polka"? How odd to comment, "I have to force myself now to go to see John whom I love." Or, "My duty is to eat this steak."

We move back as spontaneously from pain as we move towards pleasure. This is very normal. Pain is not something which we go out consciously to search out, even if we know that we may grow through pain. To want pain is not healthy. Yet we often associate pain with having to do our duty to God or to the loved ones who depend upon us. "I'd like not to spend two hours balancing this checkbook this month but it is my duty as a father of this family, etc."

Philosophers have long told us that the pain and pleasure principles operate with us most of the time. There are some exceptions we might make to that, exceptions like birth and loving others in such a way as to invite them to grow despite or because of our pain or our pleasure.

Today's meaning falls into these categories of birth and love. Jesus walks ahead with enormous courage into pain and death. The readings indicate that he did not wish pain, recoiled from it as pain that any human would shun. He did not savor his pain as pleasurable. Some artists of the passion of Christ have presented him in a rather stoic manner as he walked to death. He perhaps knew that the way to love us was acceptance of his death. That part of his consciousness we cannot know. He wished obviously that we might love and be loved more fully. That fact is very hard to grasp: that we are loved enough to have our birth to fuller life risked at the price of death. Jesus obviously went into pain with the spontaneity of acceptance, not finding pleasure in it. Such passion is love of a sort we may not often reflect upon. Jesus apparently had no passion for pleasure nor for pain but accepted both of them in his passion for persons.

QUESTIONS FOR REFLECTION
1. Can I think of any times when pleasure was a duty for me?
2. Does pain seem to be a duty I live through?
3. Would the attitude of "suffering for others" as today's feast might indicate always or ever be healthy for me?
4. What meaning do you find in calling this "Passion" Sunday?
5. Where do I see the Passion of Christ today?

SCRIPTURE READING Cycle A (*Matthew 26:14-27:66*)
Cycle B (*Mark 15:1-39*) Cycle C (*Luke 22:14-23:56*)

My resolution: _____

APPRECIATION OF SCRIPTURE
1 ASH WEDNESDAY
Mary Maher

EVENT: **THE HEART OF RELIGION**
Glenn sat slumped over the dining room table. His face was white, drawn and the 86 years of age which were accredited to his life seemed a burden now impossible to bear. He sobbed with the kind of restraint with which men learn to sob in our society. Leila, his sister-in-law, put her arm around him to rest it over his long bony shoulder. "It will be all right, Glenn. Mary and I will take you back with us to the lake. We will not leave you alone. Florence would not want that nor would we. She

knew that you liked the Duluth lake. Come on now; things will get better. We will all help. Your niece will be here soon, too."

Mary, moving from the sofa towards the table, said, "C'mon, Smitty, we have to go see if those vitamin pills you take are really what the doctor wants you to take. We can't have you taking poultry medicine even if you are an old bird."

Glenn lifted his head and smiled wearily at his sister-in-law. "Kid, I know those pills are right but if you worry I'll go."

"Wait, Glenn, here is a letter from your brother. Shall I read it to you?"

"Dear Glenn. I am sorry to hear of Florence's death. I hope that you can find a place to live. You ought not to live alone. I can't come now but I will try to get there in the fall. Irma has a bad vein in her leg and the trip from California would be too long for her. So I decided not to come, too. God will take care of you. I will see you in a few months and until then I will pray for you. Love, Joe."

Glenn stared at the letter as if it were a blank piece of paper and said with a half-audible voice, "He would never have come."

Mary grabbed the arm of the old man and demanded, "O.K., Smitty, Let's go. Let's go before you get stubborn again."

Glenn smiled and let his cigar ashes spark against his neat suit. "Leila, are you sure that Mary will be here for the funeral? I don't want to go to communion alone."

"Yes, she promised. You know that Marv and I just can't go, I wouldn't feel right after the divorce and that."

ATTITUDES AND IDEAS IN THE EVENT
1. Who indeed were brothers?
2. How did Joe's appeal to prayer "feel" to you?
3. Did it seem right that Mary and Leila were so unsure of themselves about Communion?
4. What Christian attitudes did you see operative in this event?
5. What attitudes seemed hollow and unredeemed?

SCRIPTURE READING   (*Matthew 6:1-6, 16-18*)

SCRIPTURE SPEAKS TO THE EVENT
1. What does a religious act really mean? Does this Scripture text say anything special to you about the nature of religion?
2. If you were Leila, how do you think you would have responded as you read this Scripture text?
3. If you were Glenn, how do you think you would have responded as you read it?
4. How would you describe the need for hiddenness in doing our deeds as it applied to the event?

My resolution: _____

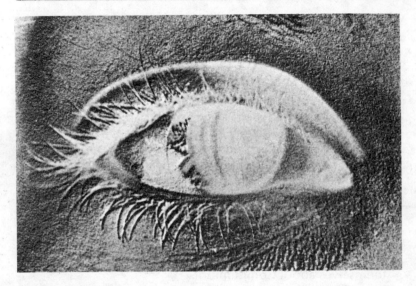

2 FIRST SUNDAY IN LENT

EVENT: **RIGHT AND JUST VALUES**

I am sitting, standing, shuffling between lines at the United Air Terminal in Washington, D.C., awaiting a friend. It is the Sunday after Thanksgiving; wind and heavy rain seem to belch in from every door that opens. I somehow recall the Eastern Christian pledge: "The glory of God is man fully alive." In this air terminal today I wonder what that means. A short fat man wearing a Coca-Cola sweatshirt shows how much he eats at every step he takes. Yet he seems so utterly at peace with this chaos. He looks so sure that something good is coming out of a snow-clogged airport. A man near me is patiently telling his two teenagers about how high crosswinds get in the air; his words and the violent example reveal him as more artist than scientist. ("Wind going up through a flute base in the air?")

A lovely South African woman talks to me of her fear of not

getting to Chicago. Misplaced madonna with child.

A woman dressed the color of her poodle both indicate the necessity of seeing him more than her.

A woman in bold reds and violet walks like a big fresh bouquet through the crowds, followed by a husband trying to locate her by shouting her name. Maybe with reason.

A college fellow, presumably, walks with his skis over his head to avoid their poking people. He looks kind. During all the confusion a middle-aged man has a heart attack so we are all pushed back to allow a stretcher out.

In the middle of all this I read the insurance advice available in the corner. It tells me the limitations of liability in air travel. I hear Chicago cursed over and over as if it were the Western hatchery of weather. A man gets one of his feet on the luggage roller belt and does a half-lotus to keep himself from breaking a limb. I hear a small child standing in the middle of this grist of milling men. She is saying. "Mommy, can we go to the ice cream machine?"

ATTITUDES AND IDEAS IN THE EVENT

1. What attitudes do you see in this event and how are they shown?
2. What attitudes seem foreign to the gospel?
3. What attitudes seem human and related to what might be gospel life?
4. Do you believe that in time of stress our true worth (righteousness, justice) comes out?
5. Do you think that the stress of this setting offered an approach to values, most especially the values of justice and righteousness?

SCRIPTURE READING Cycle A (Romans 5:12-19)

Cycle B (1 Peter 3:18-22) Cycle C (Romans 10:8-13)

SCRIPTURE SPEAKS TO THE EVENT
1. Does anything you just read in Scripture speak to the event you just read?
2. Does it say anything to support the attitudes you saw in the airport scene?
3. What do you think would be the result if suddenly this Scripture reading was read over the airport public address system?
4. Can you locate one person on the airport scene whom you think would really understand this Scripture reading?

My resolution: _____

3 SECOND SUNDAY IN LENT

EVENT: **SACRED PLACES**

"I'm glad that I am here," Eleanor thought. It had been years since she had spent any time in New Orleans. The intensity of Roy's business life seemed to sweep away so many trips they had hoped to make. Like here; they had always wanted to come back here to the church where they were married, where the children had been baptized and where the twins had received their first communion.

So many memories, so much time. How nervous Roy had been on the day of their wedding, wondering up to the time of going down the aisle if they were really going to get tickets to get on the boat for their honeymoon trip. What a grand day that was! How lovely her dress was.

Their first child had never come here. Medicine was not the same then; maybe now a child like that would have lived. But Junior and Barb and Betty—this had been their church. They were baptized here. Every day before school they came here to Mass. I wonder where the statues of angels hovering over

the baptismal font are? Well, a lot has changed in the church. Maybe it is for the better. I don't know sometimes; Barb's children seem to believe nothing.

Roy always wanted to come back here. He would have loved to see this church again. Perhaps he would laugh in his distracted way at any of my romantic preoccupations with it. But then one has a right to memories when one is older. But the changes, so many! Barb in Montana now with Ed teaching at the university. Betty again in school. I wish that her marriage had been better for her. Ted, as always, so hard to know where he really was inside. Now and again a letter from Mary saying that they were terribly busy. They were good children; we can be proud of them yet. It just seems life is harder for people now than it was for Roy and me.

The church seemed warm, friendly, a point of refuge as she sat looking around it, not remembering to do what she had always commanded her children to do: "Now you kneel and pray." Perhaps that was all she was doing anyway on this warm New Orleans afternoon: praying.

ATTITUDES AND IDEAS IN THE EVENT
1. Why does this seem a sacred place to Eleanor? Has something transformed it?
2. Locate both her remembrances of joy and of pain.
3. Has the church taken on more than the significance of a building?
4. Do you think Eleanor's children would feel at all as she does about this place?

SCRIPTURE READING
Today's reading is especially important to our Eastern Orthodox brothers and sisters. It is the reading of the transfiguration. Read it thinking of the changes which happen in it and how people in the event respond to Jesus' change.

Cycle A   (Matthew 17:1-9)

Cycle B   (Mark 9:2-9)

Cycle C   (Luke 9:28-36)

SCRIPTURE SPEAKS TO THE EVENT
1. Can you see any similarity between the event described in Scripture and what happened to Eleanor in church?
2. Obviously something more than we can grasp occurs in today's Scripture story. Is there a relationship between the events?
3. Why are places sacred to people?

My resolution: _____

4 THIRD SUNDAY IN LENT

EVENT: **FAITH SENSITIZES TO HUMAN FEELING**

Laura sat in the doctor's office. Her face was flushed and the shaking of her body against the leather seat caused the other patients to look at her. An older assured-looking gentleman asked her if she would like some coffee. She smiled her refusal faintly and took up a magazine. Pages blurred as the tears swept words into liquid form before her.

Why had John not left her more, a will to live, a will to carry on, a child, some reason? Why had he left? Maybe she was too much. He called her "a heavy trip." It was like cold acid on her tender spirit. How could John have known all that made her as she was? They had tried to talk. We were young—yes, maybe her mother was right; they were too young to marry. Yet John was so sure of his future with the agency. They could have a child; but then Janet came.

"You'll get not to fear these psychiatrists after a while." The older man rejoined her world with words. "Funny how many really good people you meet here. Just a lot of wounded people who keep hoping and sometimes just going makes them well. Some days when I go to work I feel as if people here have got things going more than others. You have to be honest here. That isn't necessary everywhere these days. Sometimes people cannot help things. I spend all my life trying to show my wife that I'm closer to things than she thinks that I am. I guess the doc may be right. She might need me sick to keep our marriage going."

Laura jolted. "She needs you sick?"

"Honey, you're young. I haven't any idea where you are at. I see that you're scared. But you learn as time goes on. It is just important to be able to tell others they can be wrong, too. That can be a funny thing about therapy. You get your head on straight or least are trying and then you have to cope with those who don't think you've even got a head. But don't worry, you're young. Things will get better."

"You want some coffee now? It ain't all that bad considering it has been on for hours."

Laura nodded yes.

ATTITUDES AND IDEAS IN THE EVENT

1. What sensitivities in Laura seem greatly wounded?
2. When wounded, do people usually blame others? Why?
3. What sensitivity did the man show to Laura and how did that seem to you? Helpful? Condescending? Concerned? Paternal?
4. Does the man seem to understand what Laura is going through?
5. Do you feel that the man helps her through her fears?

SCRIPTURE READING

In the Scripture readings we see Jesus very sensitive to the feelings of those before him. Whether in compassion, anger or understanding he is aware that people are wounded and need his feeling. Let us read the Scripture with this in mind.

Cycle A (John 4:5-42)   Cycle B   (John 2:13-25)
Cycle C (Luke 13:1-9)

SCRIPTURE SPEAKS TO THE EVENT

1. Does the way in which Jesus treats people say anything about the event that occurred in the doctor's office?
2. Was the older man understanding as Jesus was?
3. How do we feel when others reach out to accept us in our imperfection and dare to embrace our unwholeness?
4. Does a person of faith not also have a very sensitive way of relating to others?
5. Does faith sensitize us to others' feelings or not?
6. What other Scriptural events can you locate to make your point?

My resolution: _____

5 FOURTH SUNDAY IN LENT

EVENT: GOD SCAPEGOATS NONE

"You really are a loser, Esther. You can't keep a job for two months. I think you have guts to really live."

Ruth, a handsome, arrogant woman, assuredly fingered her ring. She had been born several years before Esther and things had never gone well between them. Esther had moved from house to house, her husband working at odd jobs and driving a truck.

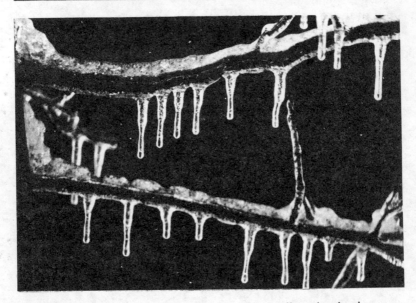

Ruth had married well, at least financially. She had never worked outside her home and had tried several times to finish her schooling. Always there had been a baby to care for or things to do. She feared the strenuous adjustment to academic life again. Lloyd had not cared if she finish. They could do without the money.

Esther answered in anger, "You always put me down, always. You have no idea of what life is like. You have all your cocoons. You venture nothing so advice is cheap. You have always put me down."

Ruth left to answer the phone. Yes, she would chair the local PTA meeting. Yes, she would try to get members to come.

Esther spoke again, "You simply have no idea of what life is really like. You have all the power you need—how can you imagine what it means to be without power?" She rubbed the edge of her jeans with nervous intensity.

ATTITUDES AND IDEAS IN THE EVENT
1. Who seems set up to be a scapegoat?
2. How do you think the sisters really feel towards each other?
3. From what the event tells of her, is Esther a loser in her own eyes?
4. Does non-conflict such as Ruth's really mean success? Is Ruth scapegoating herself?
5. How can mercy prevail between the sisters?

SCRIPTURE READING   Cycle A   *(Eph 5:8-14)*
Cycle B   *(Eph 2:4-10)*   Cycle C   *(2 Cor 5:17-21)*

SCRIPTURE SPEAKS TO THE EVENT
1. The text speaks of mercy, living in light and God's not counting our transgressions.
2. Is there any key into how these two sisters might better understand each other?
3. What would be needed to change the attitudes which have built up so much ill feeling?
4. Why does it seem that settings in human life build up where certain people are scapegoated? It is very subtle but real.
5. How could mercy and kindness again prevail in such settings?

My resolution:

6 FIFTH SUNDAY IN LENT

EVENT: **NEW LIFE**
I sat near the plane window as I came in flight from Minnesota to Washington. Tears were coming down my face so fast that I was embarrassed and faced out to the clouds. They would absorb something of how I felt. I had just stood strong

for 36 hours with my 86-year-old uncle as he broke with the strain of the unexpected death of his much younger wife. I recalled the Fort Snelling burial and the surrogated hole in the earth over which they placed her ample French body. She needed a bigger place for largess was her nature. I knew that Glenn would be taken care of but yet I wondered if new life could come out of the charcoal of these days. Would he ever have new life this side of that beyond death?

A man next to me saw my pain and began to talk. It was good. He spoke of what he did: marketing for a scientific firm in California. He was coming to Washington to present the plan for a community of people in space. This was a genuine scientific possibility by 2020, not a science fiction dream. He talked on and I relaxed. Finally he said, "Are you better now?"

"Yes." I had grown calm. "Who, I would like to know, would you take to that space community? What sort of person?"

He smiled, then laughed. But his reply was serious. "Well,

that is what we haven't figured out yet. Nor probably can. You see they have to be people capable of accepting the totally new patterns and places they will live in. If they are addicted to their present ways, they won't get along."

His words seemed so gentle. "New"—I had heard that word thousands of times in Scripture. What did it really mean? Good *News*? What new life had my aunt? Could my uncle receive new life? What new hope for so many in the world to be freed of old fears and frozen needs, addiction to patterns that dealt death in life?

The questions were more stomach-level metaphysics than I had felt for some time. They stayed with me through the night flight. As I grew calmer I felt one aspect of the answer in the man who had shared his life with me so that I was not trapped in my own grief.

ATTITUDES AND IDEAS IN THE EVENT
1. What attitudes of newness do you see in the event?
2. Is the narrator touched by newness?
3. What sort of men and women would you take into a community in space?
4. Is crisis in life likely to invite us to newness?
5. What does that term "new life" mean to you?

SCRIPTURE READING   Cycle A   (Ezechiel 37:12-14)
Cycle B   (Jeremias 31:31-34)   Cycle C   (Isaiah 43:16-21)

SCRIPTURE SPEAKS TO THE EVENT
The newness spoken of in this Scriptural reading speaks of God's action making new reality. Can you see ways in which this Scriptural text speaks to the event above?

My resolution: _____

_____

7 PASSION SUNDAY

EVENT: **DYING AND RISING IN LIFE ITSELF**

"Sorry about your baby," says the visitor who stops in. Coming from him it is O.K. He is head of the medical department of the hospital, a doctor whom I respect and love. I know what he means. He knows how I feel. He is also my mother-in-law's doctor and I can express my concern about telling her tomorrow that he has hinted of a heart condition.

It is morning now. I am in the hospital. I have a baby girl. She must be alive, since no one told me differently. The nurse says that she looks O.K. in her isolette and I can walk to see her about 10:00. I am excited. I will be able to tell if I can see her. See her, my own baby, poor darling. She doesn't seem like mine 'cause I haven't held her very long but she had red hair. I'll remember the red hair and that way I won't get mixed up. But her eyes. Her eyes.

Oh, poor little sweetheart, you really do have Down's Syndrome. Why couldn't I accept that right away? I am a nurse. I knew it was not a bad heart. But you are mine and we've got a long road to travel together. But there will be lots of people to help us.

I feel stronger today. I know it is one step at a time. But I am angry. The call to my mother and her response, "That is not so bad, it could be worse." What did I expect? Sympathy? Understanding of my feelings that I don't even know? I don't want her acceptance.

O.K., I have a child with a problem. But I AM ME, and I have faced problems before. This is a challenge. I will be the best person that I can be; I will have help from someone.

I am tired but I try to get fixed up for company. A young nurse I hardly know stops by with a cute little stuffed animal for me. I hardly know her but she understands; we don't talk about the baby. I put on some lipstick and eyeshadow. My eyes are still so swollen; I wonder if my mother-in-law will notice right away before I speak.

The doctor says that I may go home tomorrow, but that the baby will have to stay. She is still jaundiced and is receiving treatment under the lights. I can't think of leaving her now. The phone rings; it is long distance from Viet Nam, a special hook-up. It is so good to hear my husband's voice. He tells me that he knows the news and that it is not long until he can help care for Sally. Things will be O.K. I think the words of the popular song: "I know that he knows that I know that he knows."

ATTITUDES AND IDEAS IN THE EVENT

1. What sorts of feeling (death-like) can you hear in the voice of the mother? What feelings of acceptance resurrection-like?
2. What seems to get her through this kind of pain and empty-

ing of self?
3. Does faith in others offer her any help?
4. What sort of rising does the woman feel?

SCRIPTURE READING   *(Phil 2:6-11)*

SCRIPTURE SPEAKS TO THE EVENT
This is an ancient hymn which shows that the emptying of the
Lord led to his fullness. Think of what it means in relation to
ways in which you accept difficult and easy circumstances of
your life.

My resolution: _____

_____

THE SOCIAL RESPONSE OF THE GOSPEL

1 ASH WEDNESDAY

EVENT: **AMBASSADORS OF RECONCILIATION**
Only briefly are the deepest regions of the self ever known, yet
within these brief encounters we come to know the value of
love and communion. When we are in trouble, when we have
made mistakes, when we are at odds with the world, when we
have futile visions and dreams, caring for another person en-
ables us to grow, to struggle with issues and problems, to carry
out our hopes and aspirations.

Two ways in which the individual establishes significant
bonds in his relations with others are the confrontation and
the encounter. The confrontation is a meeting between persons who are involved in a conflict or controversy and who

remain together, face-to-face, until their feelings of divisiveness and alienation are resolved. The encounter is a sudden, spontaneous, intuitive meeting with another person in which there is an immediate sense of relatedness, an immediate feeling of harmony and communion. (Clark Moustakas, *Creativity and Conformity*, Princeton, N.J.: Insight Books, 1967, p. 45.)

Reconciliation is not simply making-up. It asks going into confrontations where some hard personal truths are spoken and heard. It asks encounters where the strong hands of loved ones sustain us. It asks that we do not fear healing and do not pretend that we are whole human beings. Bernanos, the great writer, says the final grace is to accept oneself, the poor, poor self with all the limits of one's life. In such acceptance richness abounds.

To be reconciled with any other person is to grow towards reconciliation with oneself. For in perceiving the personal truth about ourselves we perceive also the truth about humanity in general. We learn to know how dangerous it is to hold onto our proud, arrogant images of self for they will surely fail. We learn to know the need for mercy and concern given to us when pride rifts our lives and reveals both our humble beauty and our naked power to do evil. Before we can reconcile in much depth, we must be humbled.

To become an ambassador of reconciliation a person must have, in some degree, struggled with the terms of encountering and confronting others and thus, himself or herself. Jacob was wounded to become Israel.

ATTITUDES AND IDEAS IN THE EVENT
1. When you are truly reconciled with another person does a feeling of healing happen within you?
2. Can saying one is sorry be an easy way off the hook of real reconciliation?
3. Have you known times when reconciliation with others could not happen because you were not reconciled with yourself?
4. How do you understand the process of reconciliation? Does it begin in saying that one is truly sorry?
5. Have you ever thought of reconciliation as an act of social ministry?

SCRIPTURE READING   (2 Cor 5:20-6:2)

SCRIPTURE SPEAKS TO THE EVENT   (5 minutes)
Try to bring into our minds now the person with whom we feel most in need of being reconciled. Let us not assume that this will always mean changing our feelings toward that person. It will mean doing and wishing well for him or her in an active way.

My resolution:

2 FIRST SUNDAY IN LENT

EVENT: **THE MODERN TEMPTATION: NONE EXISTS**

It may be difficult for us to imagine Jesus undergoing temptation. Many of us have grown up with the emphasis on Jesus' divinity. Thus, the thought of Jesus really "falling under the wheel" of evil escapes our imagination. He had to win; he was God.

Many of us grew up also believing a good deal in temptation. We were sure that certain behavior was moral and certain behavior was immoral. We did not believe that we had to win simply because we were God's sons and daughters. We knew defeat and capitulation with darkness and sin. We had, in our ways, said yes to many temptations. We often tasted the darkness of unruly passion in our mouths and confessed the choice of self before God.

So for many of us Jesus may seem yet to have an insurmountable advantage: his divinity. Yet we can imagine the force which drove through his soul and sought to paralyze him. The temptation to say "yes" to the primitive greed that haunts us all was real in his life. So we are comforted by the fact that he was tempted. It gives us courage with our temptations—if we still believe in temptation.

I say that because the frame of so much morality has changed. Much of that change is clearly a help to see love instead of law as the governing force in our lives. Yet it is easy in our day to call temptations "needs" or "what we need to grow." Relative behavioral patterns such as extracurricular affairs in marriage are so common that they no longer haunt us as they did the Victorian novelists.

We have reduced the face of personal evil all the while seeing its ugly face emerge in Watergates and poverty and injustice. We have reduced much to the relativity of growth and that can gather a lot of false notions around it.

In this Jesus is clear to us, as clear as his roots in the Mosaic law: certain acts are not moral. Certain behavior throws the human spirit over parapets into darkness. Some situations ask of us that we fall down to our present gods of success and conformity and not tend the demands of justice. Colman McCarthy, a brilliant columnist for *The Washington Post,* keeps this consistent theme before our minds in whatever he writes: We must try not to adjust to the abnormalcy of so much that appears normal in our day.

This takes some doing, some real doing, and today's Scriptural reading is the base of any social and personal response we have to THE LORD. It takes a good deal of energy to discern the truth these days so temptation is not written off as simply a way to experience "a fuller life."

ATTITUDES AND IDEAS IN THE EVENT
1. Today's essay invokes thoughts about temptation and evil.

2. As you read it, try to locate areas which made you feel uneasy.
3. Is the author omitting anything?
4. What are the temptations in your life today?
5. What do you think is evil?

SCRIPTURE READING   Cycle A   *(Matthew 4:1-11)*
Cycle B   *(Mark 1:12-15)*   Cycle C   *(Luke 4:1-13)*

SCRIPTURE SPEAKS TO THE EVENT
When you pray not to be led into temptation, what do you mean?

My resolution: _____

3 SECOND SUNDAY IN LENT

EVENT: **I HOPE IN YOU FOR US**
Hope has often stood as the silent sister of the theological virtues between two oft-spoken of brothers, faith and charity. Our times have indeed liberated her to her position of equality. Hope has come of age strongly and solidly. Today's reading does not explicitly mention hope but it is bedrocked in the position the reading takes that God who has chosen his people will stay with them.

Ours is a time which has become especially aware of the need of hope. Global issues such as world survival cause us to quake at an uncertain future. Urban and rural poverty, the loneliness and alienation of so many people are stark realities dismissed only by those who choose the blindness of inhumanity. We have been called to see the injustice that prevails in the face of multi-national corporations which wield power over millions throughout our world.

When a person is called to see reality as it is, (s)he is called to hope. The first act of hope is to accept the real. It is not to accept illusion.

Not long ago I was giving a person a ride back to the college where he was studying. He commented as he looked out on the rows of jammed apartments, lapped over each other and sealed with poverty, "It's good there are poor here in Washington. It reminds the Congressmen that there are problems in our society." I jumped because I did not believe that he believed what he said. But he did. The poor should be kept poor as a token to remind us that poverty exists?

That is what I would call illusion.

Hope is not naivete nor optimism. Both of these are built upon natural traits of the human mind and transitory feelings. If the human mind lacks imagination of real facts in this world naivete will prevail. If it lacks the ability to accept those facts, it is apt to have false optimism. Hope is theological—that is exactly what it is: the logic of belief in God. Given God's power and our ability to respond to that power, people have a chance to act out their hope in evolving new structures of justice and peace. Hope acts or it is not hope. The action may be mental or physical but it is action.

Gabriel Marcel, the great philosopher of hope, put it simply this way: "I hope in you for us."

ATTITUDES AND IDEAS IN THE EVENT

1. How do you think of and experience hope every day?
2. Do you find hope an attitude and virtue which many people want today? Why is this so?
3. When do you feel that you help others to hope?
4. Have there been specific times when you felt that you had lost hope and then regained it?
5. Do people confuse hope and optimism? Does it really make any difference to make that distinction?

SCRIPTURE READING

Cycle A   (*2 Tim 1:8-10*)

Cycle B   (*Rm 8:31-34*)

Cycle C   (*Phil 3:17-4:1*)

SCRIPTURE SPEAKS TO THE EVENT

1. God promises he will stay with his people. This should be to each of us a source of great hope.
2. How do you feel God is present to you?
3. What can you do to keep your hope alive and active?
4. How is hope shared with others?

My resolution:

4 THIRD SUNDAY IN LENT

EVENT: **LIVING POOR IN SPIRIT**

How often we have heard that Jesus comes to the poor of this world. We have heard sermons on the *anawim*, God's little ones, those who depended upon him and were saved by him. Several years ago I did a master's thesis on the *anawim*. I thought as I did it that I knew who they were and what they were about. I was sure I knew what being poor in spirit was when I travelled up the high mountain in Italy which someone gave to Francis of Assisi. Francis knew what it was; I did not. I later worked in the Farm Workers medical center in the Rio Valley. I believed I saw *anawim* there; I still do.

Now that I am a bit older I have ceased to look in special places for the poor in spirit. They are all over. Riding the hot summer buses, selling flowers and fruit on the street, delivering parcels, teaching in private schools, finding meaning identities over cocktails at suburban parties. It is this finding the poor in spirit everywhere which amazes me most. They sell cosmetics to arrogant shoppers in department stores. They wait tables, write government grants, get college degrees at 35 . . .

Of course, one can insist that much patient endurance is forced upon people by the cold fact of keeping a job. True. Beneath that, however, one can ask the question: Is this endurance not one of the ways of becoming truly poor in spirit?

Today's reading commands our attention at a level critical to Christian faith awareness. Jesus came to make the powerless powerful; the cross is his symbol of power (however often that cross's meaning has been subject to the savagery of history). Losing life to find it, not being overconfident—all this may seem very unaccommodating to the American dream. Not to our Founding Fathers but to where we are now culturally. Jean Vanier, the great Canadian Christian, invites us to ask the question:

I always feel very moved when I talk about things like this because so often we find wonderful people who have been wounded and blocked off because we Christians have not lived according to Jesus. Quite frequently we find people whom the Holy Spirit is calling and who have been put off because around them there are so-called Christians who do not live as Jesus asked them to live. This is wounding; I don't say this is maddening, but it is wounding. One would like to weep sometimes because we all know that today we must radiate the poverty of Jesus: we know that if we all said to the Spirit, "Come and transform me," miracles would be done. But we are resisting. How can we break down the resistance of our hearts? Why do we resist?

ATTITUDES AND IDEAS IN THE EVENT
1. What does that term, "poor in spirit," mean to you?

2. Can you describe some one person whom you think is poor in the way that Jesus invited people to be poor?
3. Is poverty of spirit simply an inner attitude or does it invite us to act for others in a special way?
4. Do you say of any particular group of people, "I think they are poor as Jesus was"?

SCRIPTURE READING   Cycle A   (Romans 5:1-2, 5-8)
Cycle B   (1 Corinthians 1:22-25)
Cycle C   (1 Corinthians 10:1-6, 10-12)

SCRIPTURE SPEAKS TO THE EVENT
1. What is it that God expects of me?
2. Is there any way I can be "poor in spirit"?

My resolution: _____

5 FOURTH SUNDAY IN LENT

EVENT: **THE POWER IN BEING FORGIVEN**
God is kind enough to forgive us. Thus he honors who we are.

Many of us have known experiences in which we hurt others. If the person whom we hurt says, "It's O.K. You don't have to say that you are sorry," it could mean several things. It could mean that the person does forgive us because that person loves us at a very deep level. It could mean that the person does not forgive us because we really don't matter that much to him/her. Or it could mean that mistakes in behavior are expected of us. *Love Story*, the film so popular a few years ago, used the oft-quoted line, "Love means never having to say that you are sorry."

That could be the greatest put-down we could hear or the highest expression of love. It could be a great put-down because saying "I'm sorry" is a way of catharsis, of learning of "the dark brother" (Jung) within each of us and of learning ways to turn our natural propensities to do evil into strengths for others.

To be forgiven ennobles us. Far from degrading us by reminding us of our weaknesses so that we may wallow in them, forgiveness calls us into deeper levels of being. We learn through forgiveness the great power of mercy towards others and towards ourselves. As a potter is often forced to throw his clay to get air out of it lest later this air mar the form, so also we need to be thrown from time to time by how full of self we are, how unyielding we can be in the quest for our own satisfaction.

We usually associate forgiveness with imperfection. Perhaps

we may harbor the very subtle image that we are perfect. Subtle because that image allows all kinds of behavioral excuses which an image of ourselves as sinner or saint does not allow us. More clearly, if we think that we are perfect we can allow all sorts of mischief in the guise of faulty motive. If we think that we are imperfect we can do the same kind of mind-tricking except we can claim imperfection as the great common denominator of all humanity. It then becomes a swamp into which any sin can be thrown, to be, unfortunately, not disposed of.

Forgiveness lies below the pertect-imperfect dichotomy. It says that we are in a creative process, that our errors need not chain us to an uncomfortable stereotype where others are free to relate to us because "that is just the way she/he is." Forgiveness asks difference in our lives. It takes healing at deeper levels of being than we may know we have, it commands the dark moments of our experience to yield up their light and give us new life.

ATTITUDES AND IDEAS IN THE EVENT
1. When, in your life, have you felt forgiven?
2. When do you most feel the need to be forgiven?

SCRIPTURE READING   Cycle A   *(Samuel 16:1, 6-7, 10-13)*
Cycle B   *(Ephesians 2:4-10)* Cycle C   *(Luke 15:1-3, 11-32)*

SCRIPTURE SPEAKS TO THE EVENT
1. What is the attitude of God our father towards us when we need forgiveness?
2. For what do I need to forgive myself?
3. For what do I need to ask another's forgiveness?

My resolution:

6 FIFTH SUNDAY IN LENT

EVENT: **GETTING INVOLVED IS SO MESSY**

We may or may not agree that we are the sum total of our actions. Sometimes, as St. Paul said, we desire to act but we just
cannot get around to it. We would like to think there is more
to us than our actions tell others. And there is of course.

But it doesn't leave us totally off the hook. The beatitudes
which Christ gave to us through his public ministry and the
early ministry of the Church make it clear that what we do to
anyone else we do to him. That equation is very meaty material
for the human spirit. "I was hungry and you had food; I was
homeless and you had home; I was emotionally messed up
and you were coming along on level emotional land" and
"What did you do for me? For as you did for me in them you
did to me."

It can be messy to feed the hungry. Consider Dorothy Day and her years of work in the New York City Bowery. Or recall what might happen if one wrote to a newspaper protesting a bureaucratic injustice. Others will talk; that fact is inevitable.

Fear of doing beatitude is more subtle than first awarenesses indicate. Sometimes we wrap ourselves away from others' needs and call that wrapping other things: "I'm too busy" or "I have to think of the future." Fear has more names than Medusa has heads.

Yet fear of involving ourselves is like being wired in against the very growth we need by reaching out to others. We do not help others in order to help ourselves. Growth is a consequence of loving service. How often in the gospel Jesus said "Fear not." How often his presence freed others. In his resurrection he assured us that others were to go on doing what he had done; freeing others.

All of us have boundaries of endurance and limits to what we can do. Life itself demands an order that is in keeping with the direction we have chosen. It is hardly wise for a mother to abandon cooking in her own home to do a good job preparing tasty meals for the aged in her neighborhood.

The delicate question which lies before each of us is this: How can I do beatitude by breaking out of patterns of fear and helping others all the while not hurting those persons who are my first commitment?

ATTITUDES AND IDEAS IN THE EVENT
1. What first feelings does it evoke?
2. Have you known times when you felt safer bound in your own fear than really in risking going out to others?
3. Isn't there a sense of real joy in breaking out of the binding fears we have? We recall the many times when love broke through fears and we felt lovable.
4. "Getting involved with others"—what does that really mean? Will I be without protection if I do that?

SCRIPTURE READING   Cycle A   *(John 11:1-45)*
Cycle B   *(John 12:20-33)*   Cycle C   *(John 8:1-11)*

SCRIPTURE SPEAKS TO THE EVENT
1. What does Jesus say to me about getting involved; about dying to myself for others?
2. Where should I be actively involved as Jesus would?

My resolution: _____

7 PASSION SUNDAY

EVENT: **HEARING OTHERS**
An educational controversy has arisen across the United States over the reading equivalency tests. Some people contend that these tests ought to be given to every student who graduates from high school. It has seemed to many a scandal that some students at 18 years of age have graduated after 12 years of formal schooling unable to read well enough to get a job in a grocery store.

Christians are baptized to "hear" this world in relation to one yet not fulfilled. We are called to "hear" this world's potential as a kind of hope for all. What equivalency tests are there for this kind of gospel hearing? Ought Christians to demand this? Ought we demand what the gospel itself promises: healing through being heard? Jesus heard others and healed. He gave the same gift to us in the gift of his resurrection.

A religious controversy has also arisen in America over response to men such as Reverend Sun Moon, head of the Unification Church. Many have written him off as a political opportunist. But the fact of so many youth following him lifts to consciousness a vital question: What spiritual needs of modern youth does he hear or listen to which may go unheard and un-

answered in our formal religious ritual? Many of us find his doctrine bizarre. But we might address ourselves to his success in the same way that Winnie-the-Pooh asks his old grey donkey friend Eeyore the big question, "How?" How does the fundamentalist movement of our time hear youth?

The gift of hearing may be given to many of us; we may be able to really perceive what people are saying in ways they speak to us nonverbally as well as verbally. When we have been heard, in our blindness and neediness, we learn to hear others.

Healing others through hearing them may well be aided by our awareness of how needy and poor we really are.

If there were a scientific way to plug us into a machine to test how we hear our own needs and those of others, would we pass? Would our spiritual equivalency come anywhere near the level of beatitude? Would we hear the "Come, you blessed of my Father, for I was hungry . . ."? We leave liturgy every

Sunday to face the practical ways of hearing others in our families and in our friendships. People all around us need hearing. Jesus physically healed the deaf, the blind and the crippled. We call it miracle that he did so. So it is. Yet the miracle most of us knowingly or unknowingly long for is the hearing that comes when we are heard and then can hear others. That hearing includes the needs of others but also the need that each of us has to hear him/herself. We become more ourselves by admitting that wholeness lies in its process.

ATTITUDES AND IDEAS IN THE EVENT

1. How have we felt when we had something on our mind which seemed necessary to talk about and someone we loved heard us?
2. How have we felt when we really needed desperately to talk and the person we asked refused to listen? Might there have been reasons for this which were perfectly good?
3. Are there special groups of people in our society to whom we refuse to listen?
4. Have we in our own life one person whom we consider a good listener? Why?

SCRIPTURE READING   (Isaiah 50:4-7)

SCRIPTURE SPEAKS TO THE EVENT

1. How is listening to those in need related to living a Christian life?
2. To whom should I try especially to listen?

My resolution:

STILLNESS AND DISCERNMENT

1. How have you felt when we have constantly on the go or when someone needs us? Do we share our company we have found?

2. How have we felt when we are called upon to help another to be still? What have been our reactions? How do we prefer to help people?

3. Are there special groups of people that are difficult for us to listen to?

4. Have we in our own life one person whom we consider to be hard on us? Why?

SCRIPTURE READING: Isaiah 30:4-7

SCRIPTURE SPEAKS TO US TODAY

1. Show a listening to those in need related to Jesus Christian life?

2. How often should I try especially to listen?

My resolution.